Performance-Based Assessments

Also available from ASQC Quality Press

Root Cause Analysis: A Tool for Total Quality Management
Paul F. Wilson, Larry D. Dell, and Gaylord F. Anderson

Managing the Four Stages of TQM: How to Achieve
World-Class Performance
Charles N. Weaver

The Way of Strategy
William A. Levinson

The Change Agents' Handbook: A Survival Guide for Quality
Improvement Champions
David W. Hutton

Management in a Quality Environment
David Griffiths

Management by Policy: How Companies Focus Their Total Quality
Efforts to Achieve Competitive Advantage
Brendan Collins and Ernest Huge

Excellence Is a Habit: How to Avoid Quality Burnout
Thomas J. Barry

Managing the Process, the People, and Yourself
Joseph G. Werner

To request a complimentary catalog of publications,
call 800-248-1946.

Performance-Based Assessments

**External, Internal, and
Self-Assessment Tools for
Total Quality Management**

Paul F. Wilson
Richard D. Pearson

ASQC Quality Press
Milwaukee, Wisconsin

Performance-Based Assessments: External, Internal, and Self-Assessment Tools for Total Quality Management
Paul F. Wilson and Richard D. Pearson

Library of Congress Cataloging-in-Publication Data

Wilson, Paul F.
    Performance-based assessments: external, internal, and self-
assessment tools for total quality management / Paul F. Wilson,
Richard D. Pearson.
        p.   cm.
    Includes bibliographical references and index.
    ISBN 0-87389-242-9 (acid-free paper)
    1. Total quality management. 2. Performance—Evaluation.
3. Industrial productivity—Evaluation.   I. Pearson, Richard D.,
1941– .   II. Title.
HD62.15.W548 1994
658.5'62—dc20

1098765432

ISBN 0-87389-242-9

Acquisitions Editor: Susan Westergard
Project Editor: Kelley Cardinal
Production Editor: Annette Wall
Marketing Administrator: Mark Olson
Set in Stone Informal and Futura by Pecatonica Publishing Services.
Cover design by Montgomery Media, Inc.
Printed and bound by Bookcrafters, Inc.

ASQC Mission: To facilitate continuous improvement and increase customer
satisfaction by identifying, communication, and promoting the use of quality
principles, concepts, and technologies; and thereby be recognized throughout
the world as the leading authority on, and champion for, quality.

For a free copy of the ASQC Quality Press Publications Catalog, including ASQC
membership information, call 800-248-1946.

Printed in the United States of America

Printed on acid-free recycled paper

ASQC
Quality Press
611 East Wisconsin Avenue
Milwaukee, Wisconsin 53202

Contents

Foreword

During the past few years, a number of changes have taken place within the quality community. These reflect shifts in the thinking processes of both the line organizations, who own the processes, and the oversight community, which reviews them. Improvements in processes usually result in a more effective organization. Anything the evaluator reviews must be directed toward process and performance improvement.

Performance-based evaluation techniques represent the next step for the quality professional. Over the years, techniques have been developing which improve the quality of processes and products from our industries. Performance-based techniques recognize the fact that improvements can be made and costs reduced not by working harder, but by working smarter. As the quality professional changes from being a post-action-document reviewer-compliance evaluator to a real-time process improver, different thought patterns about what is important need to be addressed.

A large number of regulators and oversight organizations remain in the past with their fixation on "Did you follow all the rules?" Other departments have realized that the rules can all be followed and they can still produce an inferior product. These departments have looked for ways to improve their capability. These organizations are focusing their efforts on looking at what is important in the process and not just reviewing what was done. They are looking at "What is *being* done" and not "What was done."

By evaluating the process at its critical points, both the line organization and the oversight group are presented with opportunities to identify the conditions which lead to product improvements. This shift in thinking, from the compliance mode to the performance mode, is destined to be one of the major paradigm shifts in our history. But this shift has to take place both in line management as well as the oversight group. Once the line organization does see the increased benefit, it is usually next to impossible to go back to the old way of doing business.

I have been using these performance-based techniques since 1986 in several different capacities, and I have seen dramatic changes in a number of organizations. Some of these changes have been reflected in managers shifting from "Oh no, not you again" to "We wondered if your people could look at a process and help us improve it."

Performance-based techniques are a shift in thinking and represent a way to work smarter. They spend the reviewer's time observing what is important in a process and what makes a difference in a product. These techniques represent a win-win arrangement within the organization as line management sees the oversight team as a partner in process improvement and the quality group sees line management as an ally in the quality quest.

Chris Bosted
Acting Director, Performance Assessment Division
Department of Energy
Richland Operations Office

Preface

The purpose of this book is twofold: (1) to provide individuals and organizations with an essential tool to reach and maintain excellence, and (2) to effect continual improvement. This book examines the role of performance assessments in checking results of activities and operations. It describes the concepts of performance-based and effectiveness evaluations and the development of an appropriate mix of external, internal, and self-assessments (the EISA system). The authors further demonstrate the use of performance assessment as one of the necessary tools in developing and implementing a viable productivity and quality improvement program, such as total quality management (TQM).

The emphasis is on continual assessment (checking on results) as a means to identify effective performance as well as obvious opportunities for improvement. Readers will also develop an understanding that the combination of compliance evaluations with effectiveness and performance-based assessments will prevent problems or faults from being introduced into the system. The book will assist organizations to develop an appropriate mix of EISA.

More recently, considerable change has occurred both in the philosophy of conducting assessments and how the results should be used within organizations. For example, the concepts and techniques discussed herein closely parallel those contained in the draft Safety Guide 50-SG-QA10 (Revision 1), issued by the International Atomic Energy Agency, which is currently in the comment phase. Readers will therefore find this book useful in developing and implementing assessment programs that follow these new guidelines.

The book could be subtitled "Helping Others Succeed." It introduces a new, proactive, all-inclusive management paradigm. This new approach emphasizes that everyone's performance affects organizational success. Any productivity and quality improvement program, to be truly effective, must therefore develop and maintain the interest, awareness, and participation of all members of the organization. The methods described in the book help readers obtain a sense and measure of individual, group, and organization performance. This book will therefore be of considerable interest not only to managers and supervisors but all members of any organization.

The techniques are broadly described to ensure successful application in almost any situation. The authors have included examples to show the use of performance assessments in a wide variety of applications. In summary, this book provides practical advice on one of the more vital aspects of a TQM program: the assessment of organizational performance.

Acknowledgments

In putting together a book of this breadth, it becomes almost impossible to acknowledge all those individuals who have made significant contributions to this collective body of knowledge.

This particular book has its origins in *Root Cause Analysis: A Tool for Total Quality Management* (ASQC Quality Press, 1993), in which serious thought was first given by the authors to the new set of tools needed to effectively implement a continuous improvement program. The book contains practical insights and suggestions obtained during initial attempts at true performance-based assessments conducted at the Hanford site. Located in Washington, the Hanford site is a 540-square mile federal reservation that was once a site for nuclear weapon material production and is now undergoing extensive environmental restoration.

Application of these concepts was sponsored by Chris Bosted, Acting Director of Performance Assessment Division, Department of Energy, Richland Operations Office. Some of those tasked with making these ideas work included Steve Veitenheimer and Dave Brown, the first performance-based lead assessors at Hanford. Many others have contributed ideas and suggestions; for example, Linda Delannoy (Boeing Computer Services) provided information on case based reasoning and function point analysis. David L. Starbuck, M.D., M.S.H.A., provided the information included from Lovelace Health Systems, Albuquerque, New Mexico. The list could go on and on.

However, no list of acknowledgments would be complete without recognizing the indulgence and moral support provided by the authors' wives, Anne and Sharon, who became de facto widows during the lengthy preparation of this book. One of the authors' sons, Paul F. Wilson Jr., provided material assistance by preparing "father figures," the computer artwork used for the illustrations contained in this book.

Finally, thanks to all the special folks at ASQC Quality Press. Your encouragement, support, and assistance has made this undertaking much easier.

1

An Introduction to Performance-Based Assessments

Never promise more than you can perform.
—Publius Syrus, Maxim 528, first century B.C.

Performance-based has become an extremely popular adjective. As the prefix to almost any activity, it has become synonymous with *factual, realistic,* or *true.* Although there is broad understanding of the concept, lack of specific definition has thwarted development and impeded implementation of performance-based programs.

The problem starts with the very definition of *performance* itself. Performance includes a number of factors or aspects that, taken together, are satisfactory or not. This focus on the outcome is important, as well as the influence of previous events, conditions, and the perceptions/expectations of the observer. Consider a simple example: automobile performance. What are performance factors? The list could include fuel consumption (miles per gallon), acceleration (zero to 60 miles per hour within a certain time), road handling abilities (often subjective), driver and passenger safety, service or maintenance costs, and others. This list is deliberately incomplete; there are other factors you might add or those you choose to drop. The example is limited to a very specific class of familiar objects (automobiles), and most have a general idea of what automobile performance means. Even so, the list of potential performance factors could become lengthy. Some factors will have equal, more, less, or even no weight in certain situations or for specific users. Others may be contradictory, for example, fuel consumption and engine power. In some cases, they may be traded off against each other or some other feature, such as styling or comfort. Most of the performance factors mentioned in this example are quantifiable; in many cases, they may be relative or even highly subjective.

Some aspects of performance may be considered intrinsic— for example, belonging to the real nature, coming from within, inherent. Other factors are extrinsic—for example, dependent on external circumstances, coming from outside the item or process itself. This distinction will be important in measuring and assessing performance. The purpose of this book is to provide readers with a clear understanding of the principles essential to meaningful performance-based assessments. Describing performance-based assessments will take careful construction of a firm foundation based on general concepts followed by deliberate development of appropriate techniques. Examples of performance-based activities will help illustrate and reinforce what will amount to an accumulated, calibrated understanding. The next step will be to develop effective assessment techniques that reliably measure performance.

The Changing Nature of Assessment Activities

Total quality management (TQM) and other continuous improvement programs describe three major elements: management, performance, and assessment (also known as the plan-do-check-act cycle). While often discussed separately, in reality these elements represent a continuous cycle. The analysis of the cycle as a closed-loop system is discussed later in chapter 2. Of these major elements, assessments provide feedback of performance, operations, or progress toward goals or objectives (the plan). Timely, accurate, and constructive feedback to the planning effort closes the loop. Effective planning requires input that is accurate, timely, continuous, and, when possible, prospective in terms of suggesting needed changes (versus strictly reactive). Assessment results that are dated, imprecise, ambiguous, or not reliable indicators of performance are of little or no value.

Purely historical information is of value only when it helps explain current conditions (position) or direction. To plot a course, a navigator must know the present position and the intended destination to determine the needed direction. The current course is usually only of mild interest in explaining the present position. Shifting conditions cause many course corrections. The past is prologue; it is only the future that should really matter. Since course corrections are constantly required, accurate information on current position becomes important. In terms of organizational performance, this future destination is operational excellence; the present direction must be continually changed or improved. Only with this point of view can an organization hope to succeed. It is axiomatic that, to achieve world-class status, good enough simply isn't. Companies that are running in place will not make progress; they will almost surely lose direction and fail.

Assessments are vital position checks with suggested bearing (plan) changes included. Effective assessments are clearly an indispensable component in achieving and maintaining organizational success. Remember that most successful performances are a collaborative effort. Even the apparent success of an individual is usually due to the contributions of many others. For example, a rock singer or actor's success is dependent upon the efforts of agents, directors, sound engineers, stage hands, and others. Assessment activities should clearly recognize the importance of team play. Like a winning rowing team, all members of the organization must be pulling in unison and steer a steady, true course to the finish line. You look back to see how steady the effort has been. It also helps to look around to see how the other teams are doing. But most importantly, look ahead toward the finish line.

In like fashion, assessments measure and rate current organizational performance against goals and objectives. They also should look sideways at the competition, but most importantly forward, toward improving current performance. Based on the recognition of the value of a collaborative team effort within any organization, a new, broader management paradigm has emerged. A new management model, discussed later in this chapter, emphasizes participation and involvement of all members of an organization in achieving both individual and mutual objectives. This effort requires integration, the collective determination of performance improvement goals combined with accurate assessment for optimization. Each member of the team must measure and rate his or her own performance in relation to not only his or her own goals, but the group's goals and objectives.

This revised concept of assessment activities, with its emphasis on continuous improvement, suggests the subtitle of this book might be "Helping Others Succeed." Those less inclined toward altruism should realize that when the team (organization) wins, they do too. Assessment strategies and results need to concentrate on this positive, prospective, collaborative approach.

There are those who suggest that any form of performance assessment is, of and by itself, counterindicated and inherently negative. When performance-based assessments (or any other type, for that matter) are subjective, reactive, or nonquantifiable, this criticism is warranted. Assessments are not a recent innovation. History books mention individuals and groups (overseers) whose sole purpose was to overview activities and then report their findings to others. The considerable distaste of many to assessments in general is rooted in the previous, traditional emphasis on compliance and conformity. Another common use of the term *assess* relates to property valuation and taxes. With either the notion of someone looking over your shoulder, waiting for your first mistake, or reaching for your wallet, it is not surprising that assessments and overview activities are generally regarded with distaste or suspicion. The initial, adverse reaction to the term itself has been reinforced by previous, negative, compliance-oriented audits or surveillances. This generated the caustic anecdote of the auditor opening by saying "We're here to help you" with the auditee replying "We welcome your efforts." Based on the newer, prospective approach described in this book, we hope to change this view by showing how the results of meaningful, constructive effectiveness and performance-based assessments can result in continuous organizational improvement. We can make the previously described auditor/auditee narrative accurate, rather than facetious or comical.

Definitions

Throughout this book *assessments* will be synonymous with *assessment, audit, appraisal,* and *surveillance*. For reference purposes, a few definitions are provided here.

- Assessment: An estimate or determination of the significance, importance, or value of something.
  (The ASQC Quality Auditing Technical Committee)

- Audit: A planned, independent, and documented assessment to determine whether agreed-upon requirements are being met.
  (The ASQC Quality Auditing Technical Committee)

- Quality audit: A systematic and independent examination and evaluation to determine whether quality activities and results comply with planned arrangements and whether these arrangements are implemented effectively and are suitable to achieve objectives.
  (ANSI/ASQC Q1-1986, *Generic Guidelines for Auditing Quality Systems*)

- Quality surveillance: The continuing monitoring and verification of the status of procedures, methods, conditions, products, processes, and services and the analysis of records in relation to stated references to ensure that requirements for quality are being met.
  (ANSI/ASQC Q1-1986, *Generic Guidelines for Auditing Quality Systems*)

From this list, it is clear that the only real difference among these activities lies in their formality or duration. Variation also occurs from one organization to another. Some organizations conduct surveillances with scope and complexity that would be the envy of another organization's formal auditors.

Regardless of the nature or format, the principles discussed in this book apply to all. The eventual use of the tool is far more important than its precise nature or definition.

If the intended use of the assessment is performance improvement, then the assessment should accurately measure performance. There must be agreement on what performance is, how to measure it, and how to use the results to devise effective means for improvement.

Performance-based techniques were originally developed for hardware inspections and training/education, where their application is relatively straightforward. However, these techniques may be adapted to other, "softer" processes/activities such as services, projects, and programs. To date, compliance only or compliance plus effectiveness assessments have been used to evaluate these activities. Services, not manufacturing, are the fastest growing economy segment. By 1950, services employed only about half of all American workers. This has grown to more than three quarters of all workers. This trend, expected to continue, suggests we must improve the efficiency and quality of services. Although compliance assessments have been used in structured environments such as manufacturing, garnering improvements in the less-structured service arena requires a different approach. This is but one area where performance-based assessments are likely to produce great benefit. The differences between compliance, compliance plus effectiveness, and true performance-based assessments are briefly discussed here as well as in further detail in chapter 3.

Overview activities, including audits, assessments, reviews, and surveillances, are part of the management process within most organizations. The exact nature, focus, and definition of these activities varies by organization. There are also considerable differences in the formality, level of planning, conduct, and eventual use of the results.

Compliance overviews verify adherence to policies, plans, procedures, milestones, budget, or other predetermined requirements. They are easily distinguished by this characteristic. Compliance-based assessments typically result in a listing of those items or areas observed which do not meet these predetermined requirements. The embedded assumption in compliance-based assessments is that meeting these requirements, of and by itself, is sufficient and adequate. This may not be true.

Recognizing the potential error in accepting the norm or expected value, overview activities have more recently included an additional step, the assessment of the effectiveness of the system, activity, or process. While the definition of effectiveness varies by organization, these types of assessments imply evaluation beyond compliance issues. Compliance plus effectiveness assessments provide a more relative evaluation than the absolute go-no go approach dictated by strict conformance. In fairness, compliance plus effectiveness or performance-based assessments can also suffer from a norm-based comparison. However, it is less likely to occur. What is more likely to occur is a less-than-adequate judgment of effectiveness, rooted in organizational inertia. Many assessors, not exactly knowing what else to say, comment that the system appears effective. No basis or criteria is given for this conclusion; rarely is any asked for.

Compliance plus effectiveness overview activities, properly conducted, require technical/program specialists or subject matter experts (SMEs). The effectiveness portion of the evaluation should include qualitative or technical judgment. Observations related to effectiveness are broader than the compliance (only) issues and are more oriented toward program, process, or activity changes. While the assessment focuses on the effectiveness of the system, performance may be indirectly addressed or inferred.

One important difference between an effectiveness and performance-based evaluation lies in the nature of the comparison itself. A simple closed-loop (feedback) system is used to illustrate this. The loop consists of an input, a process, and a resulting output. At the output, a measure taken is compared with the desired operating point. This model applies to any process or activity. The model is usually described as a manufacturing process, where the input is the raw materials, the process is manufacturing, and the finished goods are the output. In service industries, the input is the customer request (or other initiating event), the process is the activity itself,

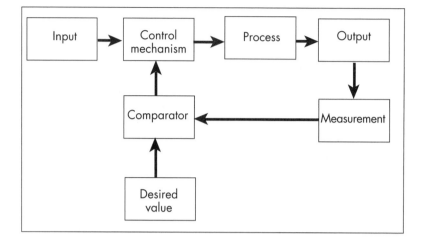

Figure 1.1
Simplified process diagram.

and the completed transaction or service is the output (see Figure 1.1).

Viewing your particular process or activity using this model will aid in understanding how the overall system works. For example, to gain the clearest insight into the type of assessment conducted, the nature of the feedback can be examined. If the process or activities are compared with predetermined requirements, then the assessment (and subsequent control of the process or activity) is one of compliance. If the comparison also includes an evaluation of overall system effectiveness, then the assessment is based on compliance plus effectiveness. However, a fully compliant and highly effective organization may still require further targeting. The performance-based assessment will examine the process thoroughly, identifying opportunities for improvement. Improvement may be identified for the design, manufacturing, in-process transfer, or a combination of these and other factors.

In like fashion, identifying the source of the feedback is useful in determining whether the assessment is internal or external. An organization must ensure that the needed inputs (all appropriate expectations) on which to base continuous improvement are included. This is achieved by the right mix of external, internal, and self assessments (EISA). These are used in conjunction with some of the other tools described in the next section. All critical components need to be in place and functioning properly. Until then, organizations will find it difficult to develop and implement an effective total quality or continuous improvement program. A firm foundation is first needed.

Performance-Based Assessments and TQM

Many companies want to jump on the TQM bandwagon. They immediately assign the development and implementation of the TQM program to the quality manager. After all, the title includes the word *quality*, doesn't it? Other organizations, responding to the touchy-feely aspects, assign prime responsibility to the human resource manager. In reality, everyone within the organization, in his or her own day-to-day activities, should be the prime sponsor, developer, and implementer of a continuous improvement program. While a champion is often named, progress will be slow until everyone buys into the program. In many cases, a revised job description, including ownership and responsibility for quality and performance, would serve as a much needed catalyst for improvement.

Organizations are gradually realizing that quality was *never* the sole responsibility of the quality manager, nor the inspectors or auditors. Quality problems are, in fact, the problems of the operations and activities managers, the financial and marketing managers, in short, all managers. Further, since most problems involve the whole organization, they affect every member thereof. The quality manager's role is reporting and (hopefully) helping to fix problems. In a well-run organization, the quality manager's job is the easiest since everyone else is doing the right thing right the first time. His or her job is like the famous repairman on TV who has nothing to do because the machines never fail. In other situations, placing sole responsibility for the program with the human resource people have been spectacular failures. While skilled in certain aspects, human resource personnel are usually inadequate in technical knowledge and process understanding. They, as well as any other single group, usually lack the analytical skills to provide the complete solution required.

Another often overlooked feature of TQM and other continuous improvement programs is productivity. Everyone *knows* productivity and quality are inextricably linked. Improved quality and increased productivity go together as do targeted performance and client satisfaction. So, perhaps the title of this concept should be Total Quality, Productivity, Management, Effectiveness, and Overall Performance Improvement Resulting in Client Satisfaction Program (TQPMEOPIRICSP for short). Admittedly this acronym may not catch on, but it more clearly describes what the program is really all about. TQM is about organizational performance. Performance-based assessments are one of the necessary tools to set up an effective TQM program. But not the only one.

TQM has been summarized as doing the right thing right the first time. This basic predisposition should be part of planning and performance of all activities and operations. TQM focuses on achieving customer satisfaction. A key concept of TQM is that of continually exceeding, rather than simply meeting, customer expectations. Top management support, direction, and commitment are obviously vital to the development and implementation of an effective TQM program. Beyond this commitment, the program also requires that certain elements be in place and designed to complement each other.

Other elements needed to carry out an effective TQM program include

- A means of defining customer expectations and translating these into realistic goals and objectives
- Using, developing, and empowering employees; treating these resources as capital
- Planning and espousing continuous improvement
- Developing and carrying out effective project and process management

- Appropriate quantitative measurement techniques for status reporting and analysis of both positive and negative trends
- An effective root cause analysis system to identify the real causes for organizational problems and identify the most obvious candidates for improvement
- Positive fault correction; practical corrective, adaptive, and preventive actions

These pieces, depicted in Figure 1.2, solve the TQM puzzle.

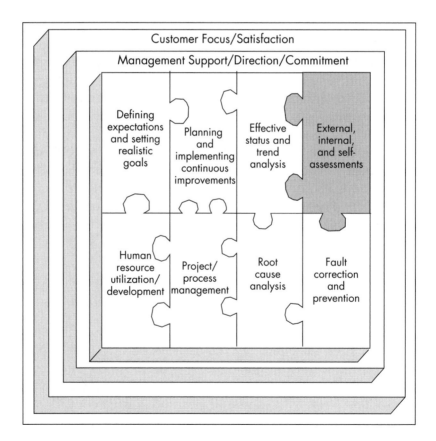

Figure 1.2
Elements of TQM.

Some might argue that, if a TQM program was totally effective, those elements that focus on problems are not necessary. That these same techniques can be used in the prospective or forward-looking mode to prevent problems from being introduced into the system is overlooked.

Many readers will note that the previous list of elements is markedly different from the seven tools of quality control (control charts, Pareto diagrams, flowcharting, and so on) promoted by many as the tools to construct a TQM program. Admittedly, these tools, combined with considerable enthusiasm, are probably adequate to solve minor or simple problems. However, the magnificent seven are not equal to the larger, more complex issues involved in the development and implementation of a TQM program. The simple truth is that these traditional tools, originally developed for quality control, later adapted and (only superficially) modified for quality assurance, are stretched beyond their intended useful purpose. For example, it is difficult to imagine any meaningful improvement effort being launched without first performing root cause analyses to learn the real reasons for organizational problems or to identify current obstacles to improvement. The root cause analysis effort must integrate with an effective fault detection system (input) and a sound corrective, adaptive, and preventive action system (output). The development of more appropriate, powerful TQM-specific tools is needed. Some work along these lines has been accomplished. Much remains to be done.

Focus on Opportunities for Improvement

Throughout this book, the positive, prospective use of assessments is stressed. There are different levels at which a particular organization might be now operating. The first level consists of the identification and correction of *most* performance problems, with some still washing downstream. Unfortunately downstream are internal and external customers.

The second level or plateau consists of organizations finding and fixing performance problems so they do not recur.

Fewer and fewer problems eventually find their way to clients and customers. Sooner or later, the organization will catch up with these surfaced problems and reasonably expect to maintain its present position with minimal effort.

Organizations often direct considerable attention to a defense-in-depth program; this is a typical second plateau tactic. However, it is a losing strategy that should be considered only when necessary. First, its title suggests its weakness; it is basically a defensive (reactive) strategy. The argument is that, with added defenses, we can protect against problems or unwanted conditions. But rather than defend against problems, take the offense. Become prospective, eliminate the problems and their source. You don't need to defend against something that doesn't exist. Remember the saying: The best defense is a good offense. Which leads us to the next level or plateau.

The third level is that in which the organization looks to *prevent* problems or faults. In this prospective mode, problems are not introduced into the system. Since they do not occur, they do not need fixing. Things are simply done right the first time. The organization uses effective performance assessments to identify and prevent problems. This organization has reached the third and final plateau that all organizations should strive for.

The New Management Paradigm

To reach this desired operational plateau, the organization will need to recognize and eventually adopt a newer management paradigm or model. This model is founded on effective, collaborative effort by all members of the team. Management, in the traditional sense of the term, is a member of this team, with well-defined responsibilities. However, the previous definition of planning, directing, organizing, and controlling as management activities is redirected to the newer, more positive role imperatives shown in Figure 1.3.

Traditional	Planning	Directing	Organizing	Controlling
Newer concepts	Creating a vision, futuring, setting goals and overall objectives	Aiming, focusing, prompting action, encouraging, persuading	Removing barriers and roadblocks, facilitating, allocating resources	Checking results, identifying improvements

Figure 1.3
The new management paradigm.

Throughout this book, *management* refers to individuals, groups, and organizations. Every member of the organization is considered a manager, whether titled or not. Each of us manages our own work (and sometimes that of others). To fit this new model, we will show how assessments are used both positively and prospectively. Assessments are used to foster improved performance and to identify and eliminate barriers to desired results. However, these assessments, like a mirror, often display an unflattering image. An effective performance-based assessment may tell a story nobody wants to hear. We can either kill the bearer of bad news or listen to the truth, however painful it may be. The corporate culture needs to attune itself to accepting accurate input, analyzing the information, and then developing and implementing any needed improvement.

Role of Corporate Culture

Corporate culture is broadly described as collective skills, shared values, and beliefs. It is evidenced by organizational policies, performance, established norms, and limits of behavior. Corporate culture often appears static, since it sometimes changes slowly. This phenomenon is referred to from time to time in this book as *corporate inertia*. Remember the definition of inertia from your high school physics class: A body at rest tends to stay at rest while a body in motion tends to stay in motion. Although corporate inertia is often a barrier to change, once it gets moving, it can be a plus feature. The corporation then tends to stay in motion.

The culture may be strong or weak relative to its influence on performance. Undue emphasis is often placed on conformance to established norms, rather than innovation. Norm-based, rather than criteria-referenced or performance-based, strategies are probably the most insidious concept ever fostered. Witness the effect this has had on basic education, where emphasis on the norm has produced increasingly less suitable product (graduates), effectively transferring substantial training requirements to hiring organizations. Talk about problems washing downstream. Until the educational system returns to the former criteria-referenced approach, no amount of fine-tuning the present situation will ever produce meaningful results. Performance-based concepts are desperately needed.

Continuous improvement requires the constant upgrade of previously accepted minimal performance standards. Meaningful assessments of performance are therefore a vital part of this improvement cycle.

The corporate culture must first recognize this need for and then encourage continuous improvement. Performance assessments are necessary to measure and evaluate progress toward goals and objectives. A corporate culture that emphasizes conformity, hinders innovation, discourages bad news, or fails to recognize problems is a poor medium for the growth of an effective quality and productivity improvement program. Yet it is these organizations that need it the most. Rather than dwell on these negative aspects, we will try to provide readers with positive suggestions to encourage an appropriate corporate culture.

Recognizing the real need for improvement may require a complete culture change in certain organizations. Change, by its nature, can either induce or reduce stress. We hope to achieve the latter result. We also hope to convince readers that most individuals and organizations could do better. However, like an alcoholic, not much progress will be made until there is recognition that the problem(s) exist.

Attitudes will require revision. Managing by results must be replaced by leading with methods. Participation and commitment must substitute for authority and control. The focus must be on customers and continuous improvement, not the job and maintaining the status quo. Teamwork is the only way to achieve excellence.

A Look Ahead

Succeeding chapters will develop ideas of compliance, compliance plus effectiveness, and performance-based assessments. We will continue to examine performance and its measurement and evaluation criteria. We will look at various aspects of assessment or overview activities to gain perspective and understand their particular function. Most of all, we will focus on how to use these and other tools to produce organizational improvement.

Meaningful and constructive performance-based assessments will require high caliber personnel trained in these techniques. Personnel familiar with the previous compliance (only) assessment techniques may be altogether unsuitable because they lack the necessary perspective or do not have sufficient technical/operations background or experience. Performance-based assessment personnel need to develop an understanding of basic techniques to initiate a viable assessment strategy, find the most appropriate vehicle, interpret the results, and frame positive recommendations.

This is exactly what this book is about. It will discuss performance-based assessments as a tool for improvement using a team approach to organizational effectiveness. It will help readers decide the best mix of EISA. The book will also show how to clearly identify performance problems and how to develop a realistic action plan for improvement. It will then look at how to carry out the plan, follow up, and respond to needed changes. Each section will describe the techniques and discuss their advantages and disadvantages.

This book will provide a balanced presentation of performance assessments to allow all members of the organization, not just first-line supervisors and managers, to benefit from its reading. It should therefore be useful as a reference and guide for anyone interested in individual, group, and organizational performance improvement.

2

The Management System

Each honest calling, each walk of life, has its own elite,
its own aristocracy based on excellence of performance
  —James Bryant Conant, Baccalaureate sermon, June 16, 1940

Numerous improvement programs have been introduced over the years, whose objectives were to reduce the number of defects produced and emphasize the value of defect-free processes or performance. These programs include: zero defects, quality circles, professional results in daily efforts (PRIDE), and, of course most recently, TQM. The basic theme of all these programs was the same: do it right the first time. Others might add defining the right job, meeting all valid requirements, and serving the needs of the customer.

The success or failure of these programs was directly related to a number of elements, including

- The clear identification of customer expectations

- The real (versus perceived) organizational commitment, especially long term

- The accurate assessment of current operations and/or processes

- The willingness to make any needed changes and to install necessary controls

- The taking of appropriate corrective, adaptive, and preventive actions to preclude recurrence of unwanted conditions

Issuing policy statements, devising slogans, putting up posters, writing commitment messages, or conducting rallies and meetings will not (by themselves) make these programs work. These activities principally indicate intention, provide the framework for plans, set broad guidelines, and stimulate interest. It is unrealistic to expect improvement without first defining the expectations, communicating these goals (sharing the vision), providing the needed tools to achieve the desired results, and then empowering employees to implement the plan. Specific, tangible goals must be set for a viable, definitive program to emerge. The organization must firmly commit to well-defined, long-term improvement objectives. An ownership attitude must be fostered by all participants, which may require a complete culture change in many situations.

Any improvement program must be installed on a firm foundation. The current literature on TQM points out the need for these front-end preparations. Recent surveys of quality assurance practitioners and managers confirm that the concept of total quality ranked first. However, these same surveys reveal that many of the tools or elements required to successfully implement an effective total quality program also ranked high (quality planning, process capability analysis, statistical control charts, and so on). Most practitioners and managers recognize that it is necessary to ensure basic systems are in place to make the program work. Without these, we have been sold a car without an engine; given the task of building a structure without tools or blueprints.

The chasm between intent and practice is proven. Surveys still report that workers perceive differences between what companies say about the importance of quality and what they actually do. There is much work to do and there are no shortcuts. Improvement implies making better, more useful or valuable, or increasing or advancing in worth or excellence. This requires an investment, both initial and ongoing. Realistic improvement plans must continually factor in the understood limitations of the current process. If targeted performance exceeds these limitations, then improvement plans must address needed changes. Process capability, variance, and performance assessments must be used in planning improvements. It is unrealistic to set improvement targets that cannot be obtained. As improvements or changes are introduced, appropriate quantitative and/or qualitative feedback measures must also be installed to measure progress and ensure that the objectives are first met and then maintained.

Any productivity or quality improvement program requires long-term organizational commitment. Putting into place the necessary components (subsystems) will take time. Additional time will be needed for these installed systems to take effect. Required modifications will also take time. It is a continual process that requires constant attention. However, once underway, it will become the individual and organization's way of doing business. (Remember the concept of organizational inertia?) For this reason, the improvement process has often been described as a journey rather than a destination, a journey that starts once the organization decides to commit to this course and whose starting point is the current operational status. Each organization will exhibit a different degree of readiness to undertake this journey, suggesting one of the first orders of business should be some sort of readiness review or self-assessment. An objective determination of current capabilities and a realistic assessment of plans and any proposed changes must be made. After all, how can you embark on this (or any other) journey if you have no concept of where you are now, where you want to go, or even what direction(s) you should take?

Lessons learned from discovered faults in current operations provide prepaid, valuable insight since they point out previous wrong turns. We can learn from mistakes when we recognize them as such and have some idea of why or how they happened. Recent surveys indicate that the top ranked employee skill is problem solving. The skills for supervisory and management personnel, generally rank problem solving after communicating management commitment, defining customer requirements, and other perceived supervisor/

manager skills. These results reinforce the traditional management concepts that problems should be solved at the lowest possible organizational level (and solved once and for all). Accurate feedback on actual performance, regardless of plans, is therefore vital to organizational improvement. The results of performance assessments, combined with effective process/project management, trend analysis, human resource development, fault correction, and root cause analysis provide the firm foundation on which to construct an impressive TQM program and virtually guarantee its eventual success.

TQM and other improvement programs are often depicted as a plan-do-check-act cycle, corresponding to the traditional management functions of planning, organizing, directing, and controlling found in many textbooks on the subject. Viewing this process as a closed-loop system aids in further understanding the role of assessments. In addition to providing valuable status information on current operations and activities, assessments are used as feedback to the planning function.

The Management Process Viewed as a System

Most texts agree that the management process consists of the following four major functions: planning, organizing, directing, and controlling. Other management models may alter these basic functions or use slightly different aspects, but this model is sufficient to develop our understanding of the process. The first step will be to characterize these functions of management and then assemble them into a system.

Performance-based or other types of assessments are usually considered part of the control function. However, since these basic management functions are highly interrelated, the results of assessments will be shown useful in the planning process and in helping identify improvements that can be made in organizational effectiveness and resource allocation.

Planning

Planning, following the newer management paradigm, involves creating a vision and futuring, which are then translated into defined organizational goals and objectives. This process applies to individuals and groups as well as the entire organization. Experience suggests that less-than-adequate planning is the prime cause of most organizational problems. Intuition suggests that lack of or less-than-adequate planning probably accounts for the majority of individual problems as well. Any planning effort should first take inventory of present skills and possible opportunities for improvement. The possible opportunities inventoried should include at least some that extend beyond the usual or obvious, that stretch capabilities, or that are innovative. An excellent example of capitalizing on present capabilities and envisioning entirely new possibilities was Frank Perdue. Chicken had traditionally been regarded as a low cost meal. An obvious improvement strategy would have been to look for ways to reduce cost since this was the framework of the problem suggested. However, a far more novel plan emerged: one that involved promoting fresh, premium quality poultry. The spectacular results required changing consumer perspective, thereby introducing entirely new possibilities.

The planning process must also be continuous. Things change. Plans made on previous information may need revision. Barriers or obstacles to improvement must be constantly identified so that they can be eliminated or avoided. Assessments, properly conducted, can recognize organizational, systematic, or program difficulties. Operational readiness and constructability reviews provide scrutiny of the status of planned or future activities. Mission planning is vital to successful space efforts. Prior to surgery, care is taken that the needed instruments are set out in advance. The examples given previously are also intended to demonstrate that an effective plan usually includes an embedded review or assessment mechanism. For example, operating room nurses routinely verify the needed surgical instruments against a checklist, that they have been sterilized and so on. Assessment techniques may also point out faults in the planning process itself.

Organizing

The second management function is organization. In TQM, this term has a broader meaning than the (usual) management decision of how to organize or who to assign. Under TQM, organizing might be more aptly termed *structuring for improved performance and effectiveness.* Our new management paradigm also suggests that organizing includes removing barriers and roadblocks, facilitating, and allocating appropriate resources.

Assessments are useful in identifying those areas, groups, approaches, or individuals that have worked better in the past. They provide baseline or historical information. The results of assessments can also be employed in a prospective, or forward-looking mode, to help identify potential problems or difficulties in proposed organizational or task accomplishment plans. For example, they may point out organizational misalignment, improper mission or functions, missing or less than adequate resource application, inadequate operational or service coverage, and so on.

Directing

The third management function is directing. Most people unfortunately view the entire process of management as this particular function. They assume that the main purpose of managers is telling others what to do. Unfortunately, this group includes many managers, who also believe this to be their most important function, with the other functions of management being far less critical. The resulting imbalance, particularly from the neglect of needed planning, often results in chaos. Since the reasons or purpose for performing activities become less obvious or logical, greater emphasis is usually placed on unquestioned authority. The final outcome is predictable. Even a benevolent autocracy approach will fail, since it violates a basic concept of TQM. Personnel must be empowered and responsible for their own work. Undue emphasis on directing is typified by the supervisor or manager who is intimately involved in just about everything. No detail is too unimportant. Another, perhaps more unwitting offender, is the supervisor or manager who worked his or her way up through the ranks. However, he or she still likes to keep his or her hands on the real problems.

These stereotypes, with their singular and inappropriate focus on this management function, are prime crisis management candidates. Crisis management is identified by any number of the following characteristics: running in place (lack of planning), confusion regarding authority and responsibility (lack of organization), and unclear expectations (lack of control). The symptoms of crisis management are easy to spot: frustrated and overworked employees, missed deadlines, constantly changing goals, and so on. While sympathy must be given to employees working in this environment, the ultimate victim will be the organization itself.

How can assessments help? Crisis management is usually prima facie evidence that the organization is in a corrective action spiral. The corrective action spiral is to individuals, groups, and organizations exactly what a tailspin is to an airplane. The eventual result can be as disastrous. There is an inability to get on with the business at hand because of the constant fixing of problems. Performance problems are not identified and corrected. Other management activities are overlooked or not accomplished. It has been observed that those who fail to learn from the lessons of history are condemned to relive them. Insight gained from previous mistakes or oversights can be gainfully employed to prevent their repetition. Learning from mistakes is admittedly a hard way to learn, but continuing to make the same mistakes is harder and far more costly. In a competitive environment, embedded inefficiencies may be the ultimate failure-producing mechanism; in certain situations, mistakes can be ultimately disastrous. There are many examples of industries struggling (and some ultimately failing) as a result of the added burden of repeated errors. One of the most reliable indicators of wasted effort is rework or repair. Often, personnel and managers routinely accept these inefficiencies or unwanted conditions. Somebody has to pay the bill and customers or clients are becoming increasingly unwilling to absorb these costs. These cost burdens, accompanied by resulting schedule delays, losses in productivity, or increased litigation are adversely impacting the competitiveness of many firms.

Whether for competitiveness or to reduce potential liabilities, improved performance becomes an imperative. While defect-free performance is theoretically possible, it is accomplished only with constant diligence. If absolute perfection is difficult to achieve, much less maintain, then continuous improvement becomes the logical alternative. However, organizations that have achieved some success in these areas cannot simply rest on their laurels. Disaster can be waiting around the next corner. There's also the added uncertainty of whether the improved (and apparently satisfactory) operations are actually good enough. Acceptance of the previous norm has several basic embedded flaws.

- The conditions that produced the current norm are static.
- The norm, if maintained, will always be satisfactory.
- There will always be sufficient time and allowances made for any corrections when they become necessary.

Acceptance of the norm is also dangerous because most people only have some vague idea of what *good enough* means. Self-direction or organizational maintenance of some level of performance must therefore include continuous improvement.

The new management paradigm introduces concepts of aiming, focusing, prompting action, encouraging, and persuading. This positive approach to directing others is not unlike being the catalyst for improvement. Resist the impulse to dictate to others what needs to be done, but subtly help others discover (if need be) and then frame the problem. This underscores the TQM concept of empowering people, allowing them to perform effectively without unnecessary constraints.

Controlling

Controlling activities, in the usual, traditional sense, means measuring the results of operations or activities against plans or predetermined standards. This definition has limited meaning, however, if these predetermined expectations are not articulated as part of an effective planning process.

There is a broader meaning of control within TQM concepts. Control must include the measurement and evaluation of effectiveness and actual performance, particularly to meeting client/customer expectations (whether internal or external). This normally includes compliance to established standards or measures, whether these are explicitly or implicitly stated. If procedures do not include either, this introduces the interesting idea that, in certain situations, it may be better that personnel do not follow procedures. Assessments provide the necessary feedback to the other management functions. Properly used, they can help reduce losses, inefficiencies, and waste and identify problems, failed practices, or procedures and other less-than-adequate conditions. To diagnose and effectively treat any malady, you should know what and where the pain is before you prescribe the pill. It is also equally important to decide when these treatments are no longer needed. Too much control is often as bad as not having enough.

Continuous improvement will inexorably cause the overall focus and competence of the organization to shift. This shift from problem solving to problem preventing will result in the best possible quality and productivity at the lowest manufacturing or service cost. The organization, once successfully launched on its continuous improvement journey, will begin to uncover and correct current operational, service, or product faults. The immediate result is that faults, now corrected, will not continue downstream to the user. To gauge the cost of problems that are swept downstream to the customer, consider that

- For every wronged customer who complains, 26 others remain silent.

- Ninety-one percent of dissatisfied customers will never purchase goods or services from you again.

- The average wronged customer will tell eight to 16 others.

- It costs about five times as much to attract new customers as it costs to keep old ones.

As the effort progresses, many of these problems are either eliminated or detected far enough in advance. This prevents their becoming major problems downstream. As the organization further develops its skills most, if not all, potential problems are eliminated from the system by careful product or operations readiness planning. Many companies are still struggling with the problem-solving stage. Others have already moved into the higher level competencies. If you are honest, you know where your organization places on this scale.

The new management paradigm introduces concepts under control such as checking results and identifying improvements. The latter needs reinforcement because the usual sense of control is constraint. While control is important to maintain stability, the desired operational or performance level must be constantly upgraded. The following discussion of management as a system will aid in understanding this concept.

Systems Approach

System concepts are particularly useful in understanding the management process. Figure 1.2, a simplified feedback system shows an input to the system, the process or activity itself, and some result or output. The output is then fed back (hence the name feedback system) and compared to a desired operating point. If a difference exists between the two, corrections are made which return the system to the desired operating level. While this represents a grossly simplified account of the system and its operation, it is sufficient for our purpose.

The model applies to most situations. The system is most often used to describe continuous activities such as manufacturing. The input is raw materials, the manufacturing activity is the process, and the output is finished goods. The desired operating level might be the production rate or quality level. For service industries, the desired operating or performance level might be some measure of customer satisfaction. The desired set point could also be market share, preference rating, growth rate, student enrollment, or any other appropriate value. The only requirement is that it is somehow quantifiable so the feedback comparison is objective.

The system can be as wide or narrow in scope as necessary. Creating this analogue or model of processes and activities helps in understanding how the overall system works. If the model faithfully replicates the system, it allows studying the process or activity using feedback system analysis techniques. Many large companies have constructed sophisticated models of their operations. These models allow them to vary inputs and learn what happens without the risk of trying these innovations on the actual process or activity itself. An excellent example of the value of these analogues is the use of dummies in testing automobile and other safety equipment and devices. Another example is control room and airplane cockpit simulators used for training plant operators and pilots to respond to emergency situations.

Systems models can easily be constructed for almost any activity or situation. For example, Lovelace Health Systems in Albuquerque, New Mexico, is currently using the model illustrated in Figure 2.1 to describe and analyze the delivery of health care services. This particular model may prove useful to other service providers by substituting *customer* where *patient* appears. The elements of this model are

- Access: How the patient gets into the system
- Assessment: Determining what the patient's needs are
- Procedure: Planning and delivering the service(s) to meet the patient's needs
- Result: Patient's outcomes or benefits from the services
- Follow-up: Review of the results and patient satisfaction

For each step in the process, Lovelace analyzes the standard of care, source of variation, and its measure to evaluate the effectiveness of the activity.

System Considerations

Feedback systems, by their nature, seek equilibrium or some steady state condition. When differences between the actual and desired condition are detected, corrections adjust the

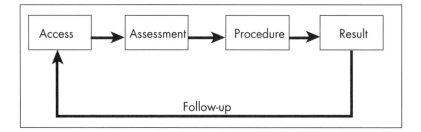

Figure 2.1
Service provider flow diagram.

process to eliminate these differences, bringing the process or activity back to the desired operating level. However, if the corrections are not sufficient, the system will not reach equilibrium. In addition, every system operates in an external environment, which also may apply additional upsets. For example, most organizations are affected by market or technology shifts. These occur outside the organization. While the organization might have reached a steady state internally, it could be in for serious problems. Shifts in these external forces can be identified through effective benchmarking efforts and predicted by long-range planning.

When analyzing a system and considering alternatives, one should recognize that compromise is often necessary. Certain risks must be assumed in the process. It is usually impractical to devise a system to deal with all possible contingencies. There are reasonable choices that prevent the system from being overwhelmed by unforeseen external changes. These same measures can prevent excessive overshoot and reduce the phenomenon called *hunting* or *cycling*, and other problems.

Management Analogy
The general management process also can be depicted as a closed-loop system (see Figure 2.2). This model or analogue is found in many management science textbooks.

The four functions of management (planning, organizing, directing, and controlling) are shown. The control function

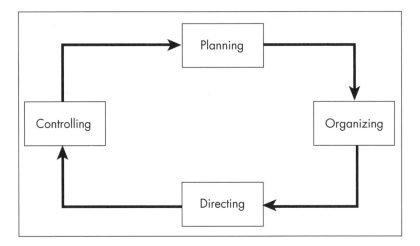

Figure 2.2
Management analogy.

feeds back to the planning process. As with other closed-loop systems, the management system is also subject to external forces. These external forces include market changes, shifts in customer expectations, the availability of needed resources, and so on. In response to these forces or by virtue of its own design or capability, there may be a failure to reach or maintain equilibrium (homeostasis). Failure to reach the desired operational or performance level may be an intrinsic system defect or the result of an overdamped situation. The time for the system to respond to change (lag) is so great that the desired set-point is never reached. Another particular phenomenon of interest is that of hunting or cycling. When hunting occurs, the management system cannot maintain equilibrium at the desired set-point, oscillating around it but unable to maintain it.

Stabilizing the Management Process
Stabilization of the management process is accomplished in two steps. The first is to determine the system lags. This is the time required to move from the current to a desired operating or performance level. This time lag results from the amount of

change and the built-in system response time. Again, systems analysis techniques will be used to describe the situation. Figure 2.3 shows underdamped, critical, and overdamped system responses. In the underdamped response, the system reacts quickly, overshoots, and then takes considerable time to settle down. In the overdamped (slow) response, the system takes much longer to reach the desired level, but does not tend to overshoot. If the system is too damped, it may never reach the desired level. In the critically damped mode, the system responds quickly, overshoots slightly, and then rapidly settles down.

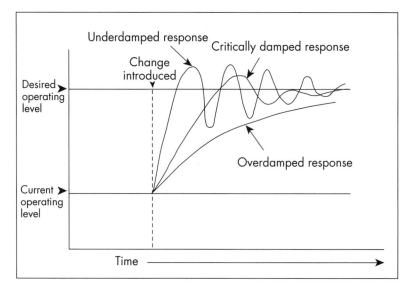

Figure 2.3
System responses.

It is not difficult to picture these responses in terms of individual and organizational performance. In control design, the preference is usually the critically damped response. This has the benefits of the faster response time (versus overdamped) and the ability to stabilize more quickly (than the underdamped). Even with the critically damped design, some over-shoot is expected and some time is needed for things to settle down. Allow for this. Different individuals and organizations have different built-in response times. In addition, the choice of control strategy itself may be different. One would expect that banks and others with fiduciary trust might prefer the more cautious, conservative (overdamped) response. High-tech or volatile service industries might choose the strategy that involves the least time for change.

Stabilization in the loop is necessary to prevent cycling (see Figure 2.4). This is accomplished by (1) clear identification of current operational problems and (2) effective root cause analysis to find the real reason for these problems to provide the permanent fix. Settling down of the system is accomplished by adopting preventive (versus corrective or adaptive) measures. It seems paradoxical that more effort will be required to solve problems, particularly when keeping up with them is difficult. However, it is the longer term perspective that is crucial.

Many organizations are overwhelmed by the problems they are expected to resolve. They spend practically all their time and energies in a catch-up mode. Running on a treadmill is good exercise, but it is different from winning a race. Much

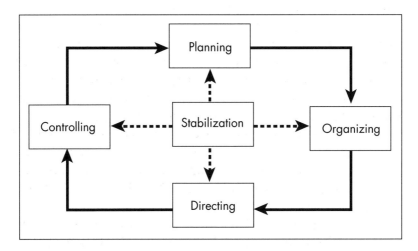

Figure 2.4
Introducing stabilization into the loop.

of this wasted effort might be avoided and applied construc- tively elsewhere. Some day it will pay off; it will result in work- ing smarter not harder.

As if this weren't enough, the set-point (desired operating level) is constantly being changed. This may be in response to external and internal improvement needs. If the organization cannot achieve equilibrium in a static situation, how will it ever do so when everything is moving? This is the challenge. The only constant is change. Ignoring this inevitability will lead to disaster. There is really no choice. Individuals and or- ganizations must strive for excellence in performance, as sug- gested in the beginning of this chapter.

The Team Approach to Organizational Effectiveness

In chapter 1, we introduced a newer management paradigm based on effective, collaborative effort. Being a member of a team requires special effort. It may run contrary to instilled personal values and may require continual recommitment to group goals. Some definition may be necessary to distinguish clearly how individual goals are melded with those of others and the collective group and organization. More companies are teaming for results. The 1993 ASQC/Gallup survey dis- closed that 80 percent of respondents reported some form of team activity at work.[1] Most (81 percent) felt their teams had a clear mission, and 82 percent felt progress toward their team's goals could be measured. Survey respondents reported team member values focused on group and organizational goals. Performance was perceived most important, with enhanced communication and the building of a culture of trust also mentioned. The relationship of an individual within an orga- nizational group is depicted in Figure 2.5. This is a traditional, egocentric model.

A more accurate depiction of an individual within an or- ganizational group is shown in Figure 2.6. This shows that a group is comprised of a number of individuals acting together. Drawn as a Venn diagram, the areas of both collaborations and differences are made clearer.

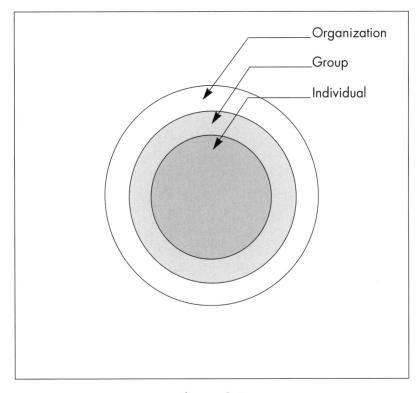

Figure 2.5
Egocentric model.

Organizations are much the same, being comprised of interrelated groups and functions. Personnel therefore act individually, as members of the group, and as components within
the organization. If there are no intersections, the group or organization is a collection of independent individuals. Because
of these increasingly complex interactions, the response times
for change will be different. Figure 2.7 illustrates this concept.

The time required for the group and eventually the entire
organization to reach the new level will be correspondingly
longer. It is important to recognize this cascade effect. It is
equally important to understand the underlying premise.
Change (improvement) starts with the individual. Through
collective individual efforts, the team or group improves and
subsequently so does the organization itself. While improve-

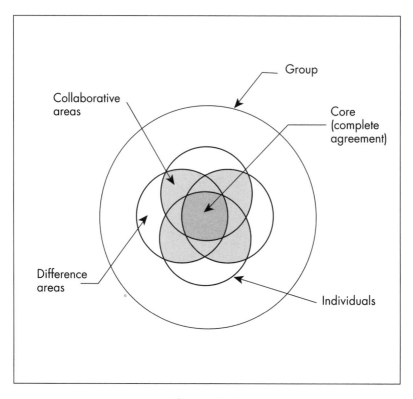

Figure 2.6
Collaborative model.

ment must have top-level support, it occurs from the bottom up. This is the place to start.

Teaming and group dynamics must be learned. Economists and futurists point out the trend to downsized, flexible organizations. A newer concept is the virtual company. These firms instantly expand their capabilities by pooling talent, expertise, and financial backing to complete a specific project.

Competitors may become temporary partners for a period. Team members may change as the project progresses. Some of these team members may be geographically distant. They may never meet face-to-face, but communicate electronically.

The newer vocabulary includes terms and phrases such as *recombinant work teams, co-destiny, core competencies, networks*

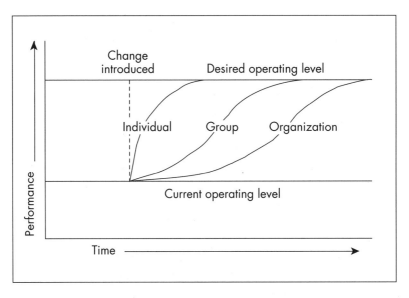

Figure 2.7
Response times.

and webs, virtual offices, portability, disposable or contingent work-ers, temporary staffers, corporate downsizing, and so on. Less than 10 years ago, contingent workers represented about a quarter of the labor force. Most futurists agree that, by the year 2000, they will be half of it. The effects on corporations will be stag-gering. Times are definitely changing.

The focusing and application of resources is part of the management function. This includes individual, group, and organizational work or activity planning, direction, perfor-mance, and control. As pointed out earlier, this may take on decidedly different meanings in the future as the nature of the workplace and work activities change. However, one aspect will always be the same. Effective organization or team man-agement results in strong performance and a shared vision of goals and objectives. Corporate culture is the collective skills, shared values, and beliefs evidenced by organizational poli-cies, performance, established norms, and limits of behavior. The culture may be a strong or weak influence on perfor-mance. There may be a need to flex current organizational constraints to allow for individual and group needs. Most companies find it worthwhile to examine their culture before launching any improvement program. There is no advantage in casting good seed onto rocky ground.

One of the ways of getting started is called *gap analysis*. Cultural gap analysis is a rather straightforward technique. The desired cultural values (for managers, employees, suppliers, and customers) are first identified. These are then compared with the current situation, any differences are noted, and needed corrective/preventive action(s) or interventions are prescribed. The technique is similar to the prospective use of change or barrier root cause analysis methods.

When examining the present culture, consider the role of rules. Rules generally imply constraints. Constraints of any sort should always be tested for necessity and reasonability. Some constraints are system imposed or intrinsic. An example would be the maximum speed of a particular vehicle. Additional intrinsic limits are introduced, for example, when the same vehicle is operated along a particular stretch of road. The constraint is now the maximum velocity at which the road can be successfully or safely negotiated. However, the posted speed limit is extrinsic, because it is set by statute at some specific value.

Recognizing the basis and nature of constraints is important in the analysis process. It is particularly important to note which extrinsic constraints have been imposed as rules.

There are time rules, such as setting working hours from 8 A.M. to 5 P.M. There are timing rules, such as a status report being due on a monthly basis. There are also place rules, which dictate where work is to be performed. There are access rules, which limit performance of activities to certain groups or individuals. Access rules are sometimes imposed as the admission to the practice of certain professions. They stipulate some minimum training or experience. At other times, these same rules limit access to otherwise competent individuals.

The list of types of rules could go on and on. When looking at rules, give particular attention to their relationship to performance. You may find that part of the current problems can be traced to rules which have the effect of being a straightjacket. They constrict movement. Some rules are changing. Other firms have entirely done away with many of the rules mentioned previously. The recommendation is: Install (and follow) rules only when absolutely necessary. Limit the number and complexity of rules. Substitute goals and objectives for rules; you'll be amazed at the results.

When the focus and emphasis is on performance and continuous improvement, individuals within the corporate culture usually respond positively. Personnel also quickly discover that reliance on others is needed to reach goals. Collaborations will naturally establish themselves. A sense of team play will spontaneously emerge. Then, simply cultivate it and watch it grow.

Note

1. *Teaming Up for Quality.* (Milwaukee, Wis.: American Society for Quality Control, 1993.).

3

Features of Assessment Activities

By the work one knows the workman.
    —Jean de la Fontaine, Fables, bk. I (1668), Fable 21

Differences Between Compliance, Effectiveness, and Performance-Based Assessments

Most readers are familiar with compliance assessments, the evaluation of items, processes, or activities against predetermined requirements; however, some definitions follow.

- Assessment/Verification: The act of reviewing, inspecting, testing, checking, conducting surveillances, auditing, or otherwise determining and documenting whether items, processes, or services meet specified requirements.[1]

- Audit: A planned and documented activity performed to determine by investigation, examination, or evaluation of objective evidence the adequacy of and compliance with established procedures, instructions, drawings, and other applicable documents, and the effectiveness of implementation.

Unthinking conformance to less-than-adequate instructions is not desirable. Consider (very literally) the following instructions given to a worker: "I'm going to hold the stake. When I nod my head, hit it with the hammer." To counter this, effectiveness evaluations were added to audits. The intent was to rationalize the assessment process, allowing auditors to comment beyond traditional compliance issues. This permitted the introduction of other criteria into the audit process. The drawback was that effectiveness was only broadly defined. Many auditors with extensive compliance backgrounds and little process/activity knowledge choose to disregard this portion of the evaluation. For others, consistent, predictable, repetitive results were considered prima facie evidence of an effective system. The previous definition of audit uses the phrase *effectiveness of implementation.* This is usually interpreted as *conformance to the prescribed system.*

Recognizing the difficulty most compliance-based auditors were having with this distinction, effectiveness audits emerged. Proponents even suggest that an effectiveness audit can be conducted separately (from compliance issues). There is an embedded flaw in this argument, as we will see later.

■ Effectiveness Audit: An analysis focusing on the product, process, and system to determine if suitable requirements were imposed and implemented, resulting in a product which meets client expectations.

Note that this definition, while better than the previous one, also folds back on itself. The evaluation is twofold: Were suitable requirements imposed and then were they implemented? The latter phrasing is very similar to the previous compliance to the system. But this definition has a better ending: "which meets client expectations." Although the prescription is still very broad, this is closer to a client-centered, performance-based approach.

Performance-based assessments could be considered part of or merely a logical extension of the effectiveness concept. However, there is benefit to clearly demarcating the three. Compliance and compliance plus effectiveness assessments retain their traditional, common usage definitions. Performance-based assessments provide the additional focusing of the effort toward client expectations and better practices. The major advantage to adopting this approach is that the three types of assessments can be planned and conducted separately or together, as needs be.

To picture this approach, see Figure 3.1. In a compliance only assessment, successes consist of results that are within the confines of the requirements (target). Figure 3.1a shows acceptable results. When effectiveness is introduced, the consistency (grouping) of the results is also important. The picture of the improved, more effective results now looks like Figure 3.1b.

While the grouping is better, the overall results may still not be exactly on target. The effective results need to be centered, as shown in Figure 3.1c. Effectiveness measures tend to be myopic. Figures 3.1b and 3.1c are equally effective. Additional focus was provided by performance-based measures.

This approach is also consistent with newer philosophies that suggest variability be first reduced, then the process centered (or shifted) to the desired operating level. This approach will also aid in focusing on the issues and developing action

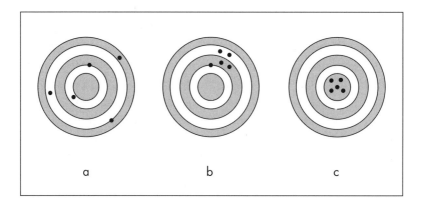

Figure 3.1
Compliance, effectiveness, and performance differences.

plans for improvement, discussed in greater detail in chapters 6 and 8.

The differences between compliance, effectiveness, and performance-based issues are illustrated by an example from the banking industry. A bank may decide to check customer service factors, such as queuing (the amount of time customers wait in lines). Improvements suggested by these studies may result in shortening the lines. In terms of this specific factor, the process is made more effective. However, unless customer expectations are clearly defined (not just assumed by the bankers), the results may be disappointing. The assumption that most people mind waiting in line may be universally true. There are people who enjoy the companionship and lengthy discussions with the teller. They might view the (improved) service as brusque. Others may be concerned that faster transactions result in a loss of accuracy, a more important factor to them. Other customers (had they been asked) might have replied that any wait in line was unacceptable. They would have instead preferred the bank install an automated teller machine or be open during different hours or on additional days. There may be enough customers with one or several of these expectations. In this case, a more effective process might still produce little or no increase in customer satisfaction.

The value of customer focus and targeted performance is the theme of *In Search of Excellence* by Tom Peters and Bob Waterman (which is definitely suggested reading).[2] The authors stress the theme that the *most* successful organizations listen to their customers. These firms act on these inputs. They do not assume what customers want or need. They do not always do what is obvious, customary, or just plain convenient. If they are not really sure what the customers want, they simply ask them. Performance that meets or exceeds customer expectations makes sense. In fact, it makes no sense whatsoever to ignore this crucial input. Be like Mayor Koch of New York City. Get out of the office, go meet your clients, and ask them "How am I doing?" Listen to what they say.

Optimal performance is defined as doing what we *should* be doing, not what we think we should be doing, what we've always done, or anything like that at all. And we need to add "in this (particular) situation." This is important because what may be appropriate in one situation may not be in another. This is more formally stated in American National Standard Q94-1987[3]

> Each element (or requirement) in a quality management system will vary in importance from one type of activity to another and from one product or service to another.
>
> In order to achieve maximum effectiveness and to satisfy customer expectations, it is essential that the quality management system be appropriate to the type of activity and to the product or service being offered.
>
> Appropriateness is defined in terms of risk, cost, and benefits. Risk and cost are interesting criteria, although negative. Benefits are defined
>
> 0.4.4.1 For the Company
>
> Consideration has to be given to increased profitability and market share.
>
> 0.4.4.2 For the Customer
>
> Consideration has to be given to reduced costs, improved fitness for use, increased satisfaction, and growth in confidence.

The truth is that when sufficient attention is given to the customer, benefits will accrue to the company without much further concern. Benefits to the customer should be listed first, to signify their importance. Focus on the benefits, rather than the negative approach of evaluating risk. Risk is defined as potential consequence combined with the probability of occurrence. Importance is the positive approach to the same concept. However, importance can be described in qualitative as well as quantitative measures. This will be covered in more detail in chapters 7 and 8. Our evolving definition now states optimal performance is doing exactly what is needed, depending on the situation and its importance.

The latter part of the definition "...depending on the situation and its importance" reflects the graded approach philosophy, which has been around for some time. As with other broadly defined concepts, it has as many specific definitions as people you ask. Those who first developed and promoted the concept of graded approach had a precise meaning in mind. It meant the application of *all* defined program control measures to a particular item, process, or activity. Gradation within some or all of these measures would depend upon the specific situation and its importance. This concept is consistent with the definition developed in the previous paragraph. However, graded approach has been incorrectly interpreted as applying *only certain* program control measures to an item, process, or activity. Perhaps the worst interpretation of all is that graded approach means applying *only certain* measures and these only partially. In far too many cases, it has become a license to do whatever you want, including nothing at all. Graded approach is another good idea made bad by practice.

Examples of Performance-Based Concepts

Specific, targeted application of criteria is illustrated by two separate examples. Both are excellent examples of the implementation of performance-based concepts. The examples are the inspection of hardware in nuclear power systems and training.

In recent years, the number of nuclear-powered steam electric generating stations under construction has substantially decreased. Many plants that were near term have either gone on line, been mothballed, or been abandoned. The overall emphasis of the nuclear power industry has correspondingly shifted from that of design and construction to operations and maintenance. The U.S. Nuclear Regulatory Commission (NRC), charged with oversight of these activities, also shifted attention from measures appropriate during the design and construction phase of a nuclear power station to those more appropriate to the operations and maintenance of the finished plant.

Aside from occasional modification, upgrade, and replacement of plant equipment and systems, the primary emphasis is now the safe, reliable operation and maintainability of existing facilities. In line with these goals, the concept of performance-based inspection techniques was developed. Science

Application International Corporation (SAIC), under contract with the U.S. NRC, developed performance-based inspection concepts and techniques. The SAIC report was issued by the NRC as NUREG/CR-5151, "Performance-based Inspections" in June 1988.

Performance-based inspection is a relatively straightforward concept. It focuses on those attributes of items, components, or systems that directly affect operability, maintainability, or safety. Not every attribute or characteristic of an item, component, or system is important to operability, safety, or maintainability. A technical (performance) assessment is required to clearly identify them. Similar expertise is required to evaluate the inspection results (if it is determined that predetermined acceptance criteria have not been met).

Performance-based concepts lend themselves well to hardware, component, or system inspections. For example, consider a valve. Attributes or characteristics important to operability, safety, or maintainability can be listed. The specific function of the valve in the system is part of this consideration since it may add (or delete) attributes. Tight shutoff is one of the generic valve operational (performance) attributes. However, tight shutoff may not be required in a particular application. This preplanning effort serves to focus the inspection effort to those attributes most important in the specific application. Pareto-like in approach, it emphasizes the significant few rather than the trivial many.

Many activities do not directly involve specific hardware items, components, or systems, but instead pertain to service, process, project, program, administrative, or management issues. To illustrate similar concepts in other areas, consider performance-based training efforts.

Performance-based training is a highly effective means of ensuring that personnel receive proper training to conduct their work safely and efficiently. It is a systematic approach to training based on tasks and the related knowledge and skills required for competent job performance. Performance-based training focuses training on the needs and requirements of a job position, much like the critical valve operational characteristics discussed previously. The following five elements are included.

1. Systematic analysis of the jobs to be performed

2. Learning objectives derived from the analysis which describe desired performance after training

3. Training design and implementation based on the learning objectives

4. Evaluation of trainee mastery of the objectives during training

5. Evaluation and revision of the training based on the performance of trained personnel in the job setting

Performance-based training starts with a job or task analysis. This analysis identifies specific job competencies. This is usually supplemented or verified by SMEs. SMEs are individuals qualified (or previously qualified) and experienced in performing a particular task. An SME also may be an individual who, by education, training, or experience, is a recognized expert on a particular subject, topic, or system.

Performance-based training has been used with success for years by the military. Anyone who has been in the armed forces remembers the targeted, hands-on approach used. Performance-based training is also used in critical applications, such as nuclear power plant operators, pilots, medical doctors, and the like. These same concepts have attracted attention by educators as well. The obvious benefit is that focus is sharp on those aspects (criteria) important or necessary for optimal performance.

Application of these performance-based techniques also provides improved coverage of processes and activities and enhanced utilization of overview resources. Problems or conditions beyond present standards are easily distinguished. Barriers to improvement can be eliminated. Assessments based on performance, versus compliance with established norms, are sure methods for continual quality and productivity enhancement. Having differentiated between compliance, effectiveness, and performance-based assessments, the next aspect is the source or type.

External, Internal, and Self-Assessments

Assessments can be one of three types: external, internal, and self. The classification is a matter of perspective.

External Assessments

External assessments are those conducted by someone other than the individual, group, or organization. Examples include quality and financial audits. These are usually performed by trained auditors who are not part of the group or organization being audited. They may be internal from a corporate viewpoint, however. Examples of external assessments to a corporation would include those by a regulatory agency, insurer, customer, and so on. External audits offer the advantage of independence of the assessor from the responsibility for the actual process or activity. The premise is that the assessor is therefore free to make reasonably objective observations and recommendations. Most traditional quality assurance programs require this sort of organizational independence. What is often neglected in this traditional approach is the obvious —that the assessors still work for the same company. Newer philosophies advocate totally independent assessments. These are performed by persons with no organizational ties whatsoever. These are sometimes called *third-party audits/ assessments.* The term is confusing because it is not clear who the third party is.

Peer reviews also fall into the category of external assessments, depending on the organizational alignment of the particular individual(s). Evaluation by peers is a highly effective verification mechanism. It has been the preferred method in academia and the scientific community for some time.

Internal Assessments

Internal assessments are performed by persons within the group or organization. Internal assessments would not, at face value, appear to offer the same objectivity as external assessments. However, this conclusion may not be warranted. Objectivity is a characteristic of any assessment. It is not guaranteed by the type. Internal assessments have considerable value. After all, who knows more about an organization than those within it. Internal assessments are an ideal vehicle for improving operations. One downside risk is that they degenerate into a listing of current complaints. Another is that they institutionalize the status quo.

A good example of an internal assessment process is quality circles. These were popular several years ago and are still used today. quality circles consisted of employees within a given organization, such as production, purchasing, sales, and so on. Through group study and analysis, recommendations were made and carried out that resulted in improved operations. However, quality circles were not always successful. In corporate cultures that did not really want employee involvement or change, they were a spectacular failure.

Some recent literature makes a distinction between independent and management assessments. Again, terminology introduces confusion. They are separate ideas. Management assessments are those performed by or for the manager of a particular group or organization. They can be internal or external. Independence usually refers to organizational alignment of the assessors. However, when used as an adjective, it is a characteristic of the assessment (like objectivity).

Self-Assessments

Self-assessment, as the name implies, is the evaluation of an individual, group, or organization by that entity itself. The sense that change is necessary or performance improved must be internalized. While others may aid in this effort, the primary motivation comes from within. Assisted or independent self-assessments are therefore contradictory. The only rational basis for an assisted self-assessment would be training, for example, helping others to succeed.

One form of self-assessment is a compliance self check. These are often performed in anticipation of some future external assessment. They also are done on a routine, periodic basis. Compliance self checks are the easiest, since the comparison is against stated requirements. Self-assessments can also include effectiveness evaluations. These can lead to system improvements. Finally, self-assessments can evaluate performance. This requires discipline and the input of others, but also provides the maximum benefit.

A self-assessment should initiate improving the situation. A properly conducted self-assessment seldom results in the conclusion that others should initiate corrective or preventive actions. The exception, of course, is when the environment or system precludes adaptive behavior. Too many self assessments turn into externally focused indictments or codified excuses. Blaming others for less-than-adequate performance is not true self-assessment.

Getting Started

Internal or self-assessments feature introspection. Program and line personnel often lack the tools necessary to perform meaningful assessments. Provided the motivation for improvement exists, personnel versed in these techniques can aid in the process. Individuals from groups within the organization who routinely perform assessments can act as facilitators. There is a fine line that must not be crossed.

Recognize that the purpose of including trained auditors or surveillance engineers in an assisted self-assessment is training. They cannot be allowed to take over. To the extent that they become directly involved, it becomes an external assessment. The reason for their participation is to help the individual or group acquire a working knowledge of techniques. It requires a special person who has patience, sufficient experience, and people skills to redirect and focus the assessment effort. They must not conduct the actual assessment, analyze the results, provide recommendations, and so on. Instead, they must act as trainers or facilitators. Control and direction rests with the line group or individual.

Initial efforts may be less than entirely satisfactory from a purely technical assessment viewpoint. Accept this. The process and associated skills will improve. If the individual or group perceives the results as its own, the aim is accurate. Motivated by even a minor success and seeing the results in terms of improvement on their own, the group members will see the advantage of the process. They will get better at it, because they see it to their benefit.

Trained auditors and surveillors should therefore enter into the effort with one of the first thoughts as to how they are going to withdraw. Properly launched, inertia will take over. Remember the parable of teaching a man how to fish. Give a man a fish and you have fed him for a day. Teach him how to fish and you have fed him for life.

Assessment Types and Approaches

The three types of assessments are largely a matter of perspective. Objectivity and independence of view are characteristics which may be evidenced in any of these types. Achieving these is admittedly more difficult when the examination is directed inward. We need the inspiration provided by Oliver Cromwell.[4]

> "Mr. Lely. I desire you would use all your skill to paint my picture truly like me, and not flatter me at all; but remark all these roughnesses, pimples, warts, and everything as you see me, otherwise I will never pay a farthing for it."

The basic approach for any type of assessment may be compliance, effectiveness, or performance-based. This is shown in Figure 3.2 which displays the variety of types and approaches available. Given these options, it is important to achieve the right mix. The mix of external, internal, and self-assessments and the types will vary *depending on the situation.* Here's that thought again. Most organizations should use all nine for the best results.

Arguments pro and con for internal versus external assessments are similar to those for inside versus outside corporate boards. These can be found in most management science texts.

	Types		
Basis	Internal	External	Self
Compliance	x	x	x
Compliance plus effectiveness	x	x	x
Performance-based	x	x	x

Figure 3.2
Matrix of assessment types and approaches.

Certain situations require a detailed insider's understanding of the operation. Others benefit greatly from having directors from varied backgrounds. There are few companies that have either exclusive insider or outsider boards. Most find a mix better. Unfortunately, there are far too many companies that rely on internal assessments alone. The predictable result is corporate myopia. However, unlike the medical equivalent, this dysfunction can be fatal to an organization.

Essential Elements of a True Performance-Based Assessment

Most practitioners agree performance-based assessments require the direct observation and evaluation of the process or activity. This minimum requirement differentiates performance-based assessments from all others.

Direct observation would seem intuitively obvious and therefore require no further discussion. However, since the subsequent evaluation is primarily based on these observations, the basis and accuracy of these observations are vitally important. The ability to discern what is really happening is crucial. This understanding is needed to focus the observation(s).

By definition, performance relates to the accomplishment of an activity or process. Obviously, if there is no process or activity underway, performance cannot be observed directly. However, performance can also be inferred from its results. This may be the only option available when the activity has already occurred, when direct observation is impractical or impossible, or when there are several acceptable methods to perform the same activity. In this situation, performance standards are not easily defined. Inferring performance from its results does not allow sufficient understanding for a meaningful evaluation. Results are just that. They do not usually yield enough information to replicate desirable performance. The distinction between direct observation of an activity or process and an inference based on observing the results involves formulating a cause-and-effect relationship. This relationship, which must be accurate, is not always easy to construct. Remember the importance of chain of custody or events crucial in legal proceedings. Problems in relating a series of activities or events, their surrounding circumstances, and eventual outcome forms the basis for the events and causal factors root cause analysis technique. The premise is that activities can be influenced by surrounding conditions, called *causal factors*. Quite often, the investigator will discover that, by itself, the sequence of events may not accurately predict the outcome. The circumstances must also be examined. Situational differences must be identified.

Consider the simple case of an automobile accident in which there is only one vehicle involved. The car skids off the road. When the police arrive, the driver is noticeably intoxicated. The obvious conclusion given the clues thus far is that the accident was caused by the driver's condition. However, the driver may have taken one or several drinks *after* the accident and not before. There may have been a slick condition, which might have caused the accident regardless of the driver's condition. The driver may have swerved to avoid an animal which leapt onto the road. There may have been a poorly posted dangerous curve or bump which temporarily caused the car to go out of control. This list of other possible factors could be expanded, but hopefully the point has been made. Unless all factors are included, conclusions can be seriously flawed, even totally inaccurate.

Performance can be judged based on job/process/activity knowledge or by compliance to appropriate procedures/standards. Evaluation based on the latter requires some caution. Uncompromising adherence to ineffective standards can result in inadequate performance. Recognizing this deficiency, informal corrections are often made. This results in an assessment in which the individual, group, or organization rates high on performance, but poorly on compliance. The development of fixes or workarounds outside the formal procedural system highlights the necessity that assessments be based on direct observation of the process. There are often elements of the process that are not documented and therefore might not be observed during a compliance assessment. Given the choice between correcting procedures or performance, the former is the more desirable condition. It is also usually easier to fix.

Performance also can be influenced by limitations and constraints imposed by the system. Where possible, the observer must understand how these may affect performance and adjust accordingly. Even an expert (or team of experts) can sometimes be misled. Observations of performance are particularly prone to unrecognized influences. An example of an unknown (at first) influence affecting performance would be the famous Hawthorne Study.[5]

Conducted during the late 1920s as part of the developing industrial engineering discipline, it took place at the Hawthorne plant owned by Western Electric in Cicero, Illinois. The study followed classical experiment guidelines. Both an experimental and control group were formed. The purpose was to learn the effects of various factors on production, such as heating, lighting, and so on. In consultation with the experimental group, lighting was increased. This resulted in improved production. Other factors were also modified. Every time one of these factors was improved, increased production also resulted. The study team was elated. It felt it had identified several factors, which, if improved, would result in increased production. It was only a matter of writing up the report and sending it to management.

Then, whether deliberately or not, the team decided to return each factor to its original condition. This would prove the results as the expected drop in production occurred. Again, in consultation with the experimental group, the team decided to reduce the lighting. Unpredictably, production rose again. Each time another factor was changed, the same unexpected result occurred. It finally occurred to the team that an unseen (confounding) factor was present. Those readers who have followed this story so far can guess what it was: direct employee involvement in decision making. This discovery was later the basis for programs such as quality circles and as an element of the more current TQM.

Situational and other performance-affecting conditions can be expected to play a more important role when performance is less strictly prescribed. Where possible, acceptable performance standards must be addressed. This is discussed further under the topic of focusing on the issues. Performance may be measured by the following basic criteria.

1. Above predefined, acceptable minimum levels, below maximum allowable limits, at some norm, or within a particular range

2. In accordance with expectations defined or implied by customers, SMEs, or other means

3. Inferred from the results obtained

4. Whether or not it meets certain standards or goals

In rating performance, cautions about using criteria 1 and 4 have already been provided. The dangers in judging performance from inferences (criterion 3) also have been discussed. This means that the majority of effective performance-based assessments concentrate on criterion 2: expectations defined or implied by customers, SMEs, or other means. This fits our previous development of what constitutes a performance-based assessment. What remains then, is to define how to obtain accurate performance measurements and how to factor in client expectations.

Obtaining Meaningful Performance Measurements

In the previous section, essential elements of performance-based assessments were described. It was established that direct observation of an activity or process was required. Problems related to cause-and-effect relationships were recognized. Finally, firm criteria, based primarily on customer expectations, need to be developed. Once performance criteria are established, measurements can be made.

Many companies will contend that they already have performance measures. These are usually called *performance indicators*. Some will add that they also trend these indicators to ensure proper operations. The truth is that most of these indicators fall short of the mark.

A simple example might be defects per 1000 units. Another might be accidents per worker-days or days without a lost-time accident. First, based on the definitions developed so far, not one of these examples is a true performance indicator. They are based on results. Performance must be inferred.

This inference may be incorrect. Most performance indicators are ratios. Ratios are funny animals. A ratio comes from two numbers. Either of these may change, leaving no real indication of what has happened. More ominously, both may change, but in the appropriate amount, so the calculated ratio will not move at all.

Let's return to the original concern. Are these examples really measures of performance? Is defects per 1000 units a reliable indicator of manufacturing operations? Let's assume the defect rate in one company is the same this period as last. The conclusion (based simply on this ratio not moving) is that things are no better or worse. However, just holding this measure constant might have required above average performance. The production rate might have tripled. There may have been severe component or material problems. Turnover of personnel may have increased. Product complexity may have changed. Substitutions may have occurred. In other words, the production department may have successfully mastered a host of other challenges while holding the defect rate constant. Alternately, this performance indicator might show improvement (fewer defects) based on circumstances having nothing whatsoever to do with the department's performance. An example would be improved components being received from the supplier.

It turns out then that what many consider performance indicators are not that at all. While some have the potential to be accurate indicators, all require careful examination to determine their accuracy in relation to performance. Considerable attention will be paid to defining focused, meaningful performance measures in chapter 6. These measures must factor in realistic, customer-focused expectations.

Factoring in Customer Expectations

We are all both customers and suppliers. Customers may be external or internal. The distinction between wants and needs must be made. All appropriate customer needs should be met or exceeded. The *appropriate* is inserted to discriminate needs by importance and the particular situation.

There are different genre of goods and services. What suffices for a toenail excision may be entirely inadequate for open-heart surgery. Consumers generally recognize that the family car is different from a LeMans racer. Expectations that exceed understandable criteria can be considered invalid. Once the list of needs is complete, performance-based criteria can be applied. Concentrate on those needs important to the particular situation. Disregard the others, unless they are somehow free. By free, we mean that sometimes you get an unexpected bonus. By meeting one requirement, you fulfill another. This doesn't happen often, but it sometimes does.

How are these expectations defined? First, if most organizations honestly and objectively listed what they *believed* their customers wanted, they would probably be 80 percent accurate. There is a downside risk in doing this. Some organizations have already lost touch with their customers. There is not much to be expected in this case. Another problem is that this list gets stated from the supply side, which again is of no practical value. However, assume a credible job was done. We have a list that may be up to 80 percent accurate. What about the other 20 percent? The answer should be clear. Ask your customer. If you decide to postpone finishing the job, at least get started on what you have. It's a start; you can always make course corrections later (see chapter 6 for more information).

What are some typical customer requirements? Naturally any listing will depend on the specific market sector and organization's business activities. However, a partial list of customer expectations would include

- Timeliness or service timing
- Accuracy (which includes repeatability and consistency)
- Clarity and precision
- Completeness or thoroughness
- Proper functioning or product safety

- Ease of use (includes usefulness and user friendliness)
- Cost
- Performance
- Reliability or maintainability

This list, although incomplete, should help in defining customer expectations. To be useful, each applicable expectation will require specific, measurable definition. This may vary with the particular situation. Benchmarking, looking at what successful firms are doing, is sometimes helpful. Do not use vague definitions when listing these requirements. Some of the expectations listed are easily quantified, for example, cost and reliability. Others are not. *User-friendliness* is an oft-used term that has no real definition. What should be the presumed skill levels for someone unfamiliar with the application or use of the product? We are all familiar with computer programs termed *user-friendly*. It turns out that many assume the user is a computer buff. *Product safety* is another less easily defined expectation. However, it can be precisely stated. Product safety can be achieved either through intrinsic or extrinsic means. In the best of possible worlds, all required safety features would be intrinsic, designed into the process or final product. Fisher-Price toys provide a good example of designed in or intrinsic product safety. Fisher-Price spends a great deal of time and effort trying to make their toys kid-proof. They purposely destroy toys to test for potential faults that might cause laceration, fragmentation, ingestion, asphyxiation, or other harmful effects. Extrinsic means, such as warning labels or usage limits, do not apply as well to children as they might to adults. Even with adults, a show of hands for those who have disengaged product safety features might be surprising. If the feature introduces a serious inconvenience, it's likely a candidate for bypassing. If the customer didn't see any added value or perceive the supposed danger in the first place, it's almost a certainty. Therefore, it's best not to make any assumptions about client expectations. It is also not necessary. With just a little effort you can find out exactly what customers expect. It's vital that you do.

Notes

1. Department of Energy, "DOE Order 5700.6C: Quality Assurance." (Washington, D.C.: Department of Energy, 21 August 1991).

2. Tom Peters and Bob Waterman, *In Search of Excellence: Lessons from America's Best-Run Companies.* (New York: Harper & Row, 1982).

3. ANSI/ASQC Q94-1987, *Quality Management and Quality System Elements—Guidelines,* Section 0.2, Organizational goals, and Section 0.44, Benefit Considerations. (Milwaukee, Wis.: ASQC, 1987).

4. Horace Walpole, *Anecdotes of Painting in England,* from *Bartlett's Familiar Quotations,* Emily Morison Beck, ed. 14th edition. (Boston: Little, Brown and Company, 1968), p. 328.

5. Hawthorne Study. This study is referenced in any number of management science textbooks.

4

Getting Started

A pint of sweat will save a gallon of blood.
—George Smith Patton Letter to Cadet George S. Patton IV

This chapter discusses how to get started on performance assessments. The importance of teamwork and an appropriate corporate culture is reemphasized. Tips on how to recognize and eliminate barriers or obstacles to improvement are also presented. The importance of preplanning and some of the tools that can be used to properly focus the effort are discussed. The overall message is hopefully clear. While many organizations will require time to adapt to these newer ideas, this is not a good reason to delay starting these efforts. Time is not on their side.

Cultivating a Teamwork Culture

Corporate culture is the collective, shared values of an organization. Many of the terms used in this definition (collective, shared, and organization) clearly suggest its nature. It is a pervasive environment within which individuals and groups function. It is the backdrop against which performance and improvement programs will be developed and carried out. These conditions influence expectations and affect all members of the organization. They can be negative, benign, or positive.

Individuals and organizations need information on what is being done right, what could be done better, as well as what is being done wrong. Otherwise, there is no feedback to measure activities. We need to know how we're doing relative to desired or optimum levels of performance, what our progress is in attaining goals. We should seek to objectively gauge customer/client satisfaction. Without this information, the organization is playing the familiar children's game of blind man's bluff. The only problem is that, in this version of the game, the stakes may be the organization's future and survival. In an increasingly competitive world, pleading *nolo contendere* (no contest) is the same as pleading guilty. Second chances are rare.

There is also an old saying that a chain is only as strong as its weakest link. It is difficult to find an individual whose actions or performance does not somehow affect the organization. Locate someone whose external or internal customers cannot be identified. It's not easy to do. The conclusion is simple. Effective performance improvement programs require that all personnel within an organization understand their purpose, develop an awareness of the aims, and develop an interest in making these programs work. They must eventually assume a participative position. The emphasis must therefore be on the development and cultivation of a proactive, customer-oriented, teamwork environment.

The newer management paradigm discussed in the previous chapter uses phrases such as *prompting action, encouraging, persuading, removing barriers and roadblocks,* and *facilitating.* The emphasis is positive and decidedly collective. Assessments need to fit these revised purposes. Performance-based assessments, in particular, target activities that influence customer expectations. Both individually and collectively, members of an organization must direct their efforts along these lines. To do this, a teamwork approach is required.

Creating a teamwork culture will not be easy. In some cases, there is too much negative history. In other organizations, inertia and the distrust of others (particularly assessors) needs to be overcome. But it must be done. The eventual survival of the organization itself depends on it.

The advice on creating a teamwork culture reflects current organizational management principles and practices. It also represents concepts refined through experience. When an organization commits to providing products and services that consistently meet or exceed customers' expectations, it also must take measures that provide confidence that these goals are achieved. Just saying something doesn't necessarily make it happen. You need to check results. To improve, the organization also must commit to ever-rising standards of performance. Excellence is a moving target. Customer expectations tend to increase, not decrease. Effective competition demands performance levels at new plateaus. All activities need to be planned, carried out, continuously assessed, and corrected as necessary to ensure continuous improvement. Defining appropriate goals, planning their effective implementation, accurately measuring the results, and analyzing performance become constant challenges.

However, these activities, when properly carried out, provide a firm, comprehensive method for effectively conducting and continually improving operations. These principles and practices apply to all aspects of organizational efforts. It is the role of organization managers to create a vision, set broad goals and overall objectives, and establish and then cultivate a teamwork environment. They must ensure these principles are integrated into all activities. Groups and individuals, working within this framework, must translate these aims to their specific situations.

Organization managers should provide necessary and proper information, resources, support, and encouragement. They must show commitment and leadership through active involvement in the development and implementation of operating standards and continuous improvement programs. All members of the organization need to understand these aims. They should be encouraged to meet or exceed current standards while recommending improvements.

Achieving these goals is the responsibility of the entire organization, from the top executives to individual contributors. Definition and consistent interpretation of performance expectations are crucial. If these expectations have not yet been stated, they need to be. Terminology should be clear. Define terms if they are vague. Personnel indoctrination should include specific expectations and appropriate definitions to ensure consistent understanding and communication. It is not sufficient to simply declare that every member of the organization is (somehow) expected to do his or her job better. Too many firms do just that and are disappointed when they do not get results. This shouldn't be a surprise. Personnel aren't quite sure what's expected of them. What they're doing now seems okay. In fact, this creates a disincentive to do any different. Why get into trouble?

The organization needs to foster a no-fault attitude toward this learning process. Personnel should freely identify needed improvements. Problems in defining the proper focus and ensuring that adequate resources are developed and allocated will occur. Difficult issues will need to be satisfactorily resolved. There will be divergence as to the best approach. A process for resolving these differences of views and opinions is needed. Since all members of the organization will be affected by the outcome, a team approach is best.

No one said improvement would be easy. Sharing the load makes it lighter, however. The alternative is stagnation and atrophy. Nobody would consciously choose this path. It follows that developing a teamwork culture is a necessity, not a choice. In chapter 2, we developed our first axiom: Performance improvement proceeds bottom up. Once started, it flows to the group and organization. If this flow is diverted or stopped altogether, the progression will obviously not occur. Until the environment or culture is opportune, efforts will be wasted. This leads to our second axiom: Only when the organizational climate is favorable will meaningful performance improvement occur.

Focusing the Efforts

A true performance-based assessment is concerned only with those attributes of products or services reflecting customer needs and expectations. For hardware items, components, or systems and certain aspects of activities, these are attributes that directly affect operability, maintainability, or safety. For services, this may be limited to customer interfaces. Neither normally requires a comprehensive examination of all possible attributes.

A performance-based assessment involves direct observation of the product in operation or the service activity. It is further only concerned with predefined characteristics. Performance-based assessments have only a peripheral interest in the adequacy of procedures or compliance thereto. This does not mean that problems may eventually not be traced to inadequate procedures or noncompliance to appropriate procedures. It does mean that the assessment concerns itself primarily with the operation or activity itself. Look at what's happening.

Performance-based assessments can be classified broadly as process, product, or system. However, a performance-based product assessment is more likely to identify opportunities to improve the design or manufacturing process. This happens because you are looking at the operation or use of the product. This gives a different perspective and additional insight. Who, in frustration, has not thought it a remarkable idea that the designer of a particular product try using it? Many years ago, one of the authors worked in a high-volume manufacturing facility. As a fledgling engineer, he assembled the first piece of each new design. This was a valuable educational experience. Although all the designs looked fine on paper, actually assembling them provided insight into a number of flaws which were not apparent. Along the same lines, how many readers would like to task some of the new car designers with changing the spark plugs or an oil filter? These routine maintenance activities used to be something you could do yourself.

Preplanning consists of the review of previous performance problems. This preplanning can aid the evaluation by identifying *potential* areas in which to direct observation activities. Existing product, service, program, or process descriptions and implementing procedures also can be reviewed for weaknesses and/or ambiguity. Actual performance will probably be less than adequate if the planning or guidance procedures affecting the activity are vague, inconsistent, or otherwise less than adequate. This is admittedly presumptive. However, the team can benefit from this familiarization effort. Evaluation of these suspect areas can be made by actual observation.

Previous performance history also can be helpful. This includes, but is not limited to

- Customer complaints

- Results of previous surveys or assessments

- Retest and rework frequencies

- Work orders (with particular attention paid to inadequate preventive maintenance, design deficiencies, and so on)

- Number (and type) of engineering changes

- Drawings or plan revisions

- Project schedule slippages, and so on

The final list will depend on the particular organization, of course. Be careful when evaluating this information. Do not assume that fault detection and reporting systems are properly focused and include appropriate data. They may not recognize the real problems. Check that the information is accurate and timely. Quite often, the output of fault detection systems is simply status and trend reports. These reports sometimes provide inadequate categorization and analysis of the information provided. If the reports have been prepared by personnel unfamiliar with the actual operation or activity, considerable accuracy can be lost. It often becomes a numbers game. Severity and importance of particular problems is neglected. A few truly significant problems is considerably worse than many negligible ones. This is not suggested by the numbers.

The team will have to weigh the nature and significance of faults reported by the detection and reporting system. The teams need to determine

- Which of these (if any) provide a sufficient level of validation as regards individual, group, or organizational performance

- Specific faults which could have a significant impact on the organization
- Aspects of activities which could be performance affecting
- If it is possible to obtain timely and accurate measurements

Recognizing Barriers

No matter how thorough the preparation and how conducive the environment, barriers to effective performance assessments exist. Many of these stem from old reactions to assessments in general. Others surface as a result of organizational inertia. Some result from the planning and conduct of the assessment itself. The latter can be avoided by proper team selection and maintaining the focus on improvement. The critical phases of a performance assessment are

- Selecting the activity to be evaluated
- Listing appropriate performance criteria
- Defining the measurement technique
- Selecting the team members

Potential barriers should be identified for each of these phases. If these are recognized and dealt with, the chances for a successful assessment increase dramatically.

Selection Criteria for Activities

Selecting activities for evaluation (and hopefully, improvement) would seem relatively straightforward. Simply select them in order of their overall importance. The difficulty in this approach lies in devising a meaningful ordering or ranking. How will importance be defined? What are any cause-and-effect relationships? If importance is replaced by organizational impact, other problems arise. Take, for example, what seems an obvious common problem denominator: cost. Most businesses and their managers easily grasp this concept. It seems an obvious common problem denominator: cost. Most would seem to be a factor quickly and easily computed. However, consider a problem which apparently results in reduced sales. Missed sales are easily quantified. However, it requires the simplifying assumption that all or some portion of these losses are attributable to this particular problem. There is a cause-and-effect relationship that needs to be validated. There is also another basic consideration. Which cost will be used? Should it be the estimated lost sales caused by the problem, the cost to fix the problem, expected cost reductions (or revenue increases) once the problem is fixed, or some other value?

Some activities are difficult to quantify in dollars. For example, what about employee or public safety issues? How are the costs of regulatory compliance measured? What is the value of goodwill? How can you quantify lost opportunities? The list of problems could go on and on. These cautions suggest that cost alone might not be sufficient in ranking potential areas for evaluation. The same care must be used when applying any criteria.

Activities requiring assessment and improvement also may be ranked in terms of their organizational priority. They can be ordered by potential results from misperformance. Activities can be graded by degree of difficulty, severity, and real or potential hazards. They can be classified by the amount of customer interface or by market exposure.

Selection criteria for assessment candidates can therefore vary widely between industries and service sectors, segments within these, and even within individual groups within organizations. Hopefully the point was made that these criteria should be carefully selected. However, initial criteria should be chosen quickly. This seemingly contradictory advice needs explanation. Do not allow the choice of assessment criteria to significantly delay starting the process. It is better to get started on valid performance assessments than to refine selection criteria. The process itself will rectify most errors made during the initial selection. One technique is to start with a group anxious to improve. A willing partner is important. Use the results as a demonstration to others. Let the successful group members be your salespeople.

Some Shortcuts

Shortcuts can be taken in deciding what to look at. There are points within operations or activities that provide the clearest insight. Borrowing something learned in basic first aid, there are several points on the human body where it is easiest to detect heartbeats. These are called *pulse points*. The most familiar one is the wrist. This idea applies to organizations. Pulse points are those particular places where operation of the system is most easily measured. Alternately, they are where most problems are likely to occur. Each firm or organization can usually identify its own pulse points. They are obvious given some thought. They are the things an experienced production line supervisor usually checks on rounds. He or she knows exactly what to look for. They provide the clearest and quickest idea of how things are going. It may only take the time to think them through and then set them down. These same points may be identified through operations analysis. However, they are most often known through experience. The seasoned production line supervisor does not look into every detail on these rounds. The specific items checked are those that, through accumulated experience, can be relied upon as indicators of performance. This is a practical application of performance-based assessments.

The concept of pulse points is similar to validation, widely used within certain industries. These techniques are routine in the pharmaceutical industry, for example. Validation involves checking product quality at predetermined points during the process. Once the finished product is made into pills or caplets, it is either acceptable or not. Talk about needing an effective zero defects program; in this case it is really all or nothing. The obvious time to find discrepancies is during the process, when there still may be opportunities for any needed corrections.

When the process or activity reaches a particular validation checkpoint and passes, it then proceeds or continues to the next, until complete. If these points are chosen carefully and the appropriate criteria applied, the source of any problem is usually easy to find. The technique is similar to hold or witness points in manufacturing or construction. When these points are properly chosen, they are useful in confirming quality or correctness. Like validation points, they also should be chosen to allow any needed correction before later processing makes it difficult or impossible.

Flowcharting, presented later in this book, is an excellent tool for analyzing activities. It can help identify the points discussed here. Experience in assessments using these tools will result in the ability to recognize them. These same techniques can be used proactively. They can be used when the process or activity sequence itself is being planned. For an organization, there are instances that suggest a need for prospective analysis. These include, but are not limited to

- Changes in the management or direct supervision
- Significant increases or decreases in staffing levels
- New or substantially revised procedures
- Recent policy changes
- New or unique programs
- Changes in problem patterns

Checking every step of certain activities or processes may be necessary. In most situations, it is not. Remember the intent is to measure performance and identify potential improvements. The assessment may show other portions of the overall process or activity that need a closer look. Conditions may also have changed over time. New techniques have been introduced. Leave these discoveries to the assessment effort. The main idea is to identify a finite number of reliable indicators of organizational, process, or activity health.

Trend analysis reports also may be used to choose improvement opportunities. However, some caution is advised. Trend analysis is at once the most often discussed and least understood technique. The definition of trend analysis is precise. It is given in any basic statistics textbook. Trend is one of the components in a time series analysis, specifically the long-term direction. It is *not* the cyclical component with which trend is sometimes confused. It is not random or chance fluctuations. Trend is also not seasonal variation. Incidentally, seasonal variation or the annual cycle is seldom if ever considered. It should be.

Trend, the underlying or long-term movement, tells you if you are heading in the right (or wrong) direction. It is not a detailed street map. The sad fact about this general misunderstanding is that, as a result, valid trend analysis is rarely performed. This results in shortsightedness. Trend analysis gives historical perspective and tells you the direction you're heading. It can help you see the light at the end of a tunnel. Sometimes this is the headlight of a freight train heading straight at you. Even this bad news can be helpful, however, if it gives you a chance to react in time.

More detail on designing assessment strategies and focusing on issues is provided in the following chapters. Regardless of exactly how these are chosen, both the assessors and those being evaluated need to understand the intended outcome. Performance assessments should accurately measure performance and identify possible improvements.

Developing the Assessment Team

Given the nurturing environment described here exists, the next step is selecting and developing the assessment team. The team must set the improvement of the activity as its primary goal. In a performance-based assessment, the team must look beyond compliance issues and evaluate both operational effectiveness and performance. This is an important consideration during team selection and development. Success will depend on the familiarity and experience of the members with the specific type of activity or program being assessed. It will also depend on their understanding of goals and expectations. The latter, one of the first planning steps in a performance-based assessment, is covered in chapter 5. Returning to the first premise, operations and technical specialists, SMEs, and others will be required as active members of the assessment team. These individuals are chosen based on their familiarity with the actual activity or process. They should also be aware of any previous or recent interpretations of stated requirements and objectives.

Not all team personnel will require formal training in assessment techniques. Lead assessors benefit from training in audit or surveillance methods, but it is not necessary. Purists will argue this training is absolutely needed. Pragmatists would argue the job knowledge is far more crucial. They might also add that the traditional compliance-oriented audit has never produced significant improvement. Our position is that the training is helpful, no more than that. Other team members only need to understand their role in the overall assessment process. All of this may sound heretical to many formal auditors. But they should recognize (1) this is previous practice (nonauditors as team members) and (2) that the discomfort is due to moving away from the more comfortable, familiar compliance-only approach. Auditors who choose to continue to practice their profession will have to recognize these substantial changes and adapt. Those who believe that the old way of conducting audits will suffice suffer the prospect of a rude awakening in a brave, new world.

The assessed individuals, groups, or organizations are the ultimate beneficiaries of the final effort. They need to understand that an effective evaluation is of value. The aim is improvement. The assessment, properly conducted, should not be protagonistic but prospective. Participation in the process makes sense. Accept the simple fact that improvement of any current activity is usually to everyone's advantage. Accept whatever honest help is offered. Remember that

> "He that wrestles with us, strengthens our nerves and sharpens our skill. Our antagonist is our helper." Edmund Burke (1729–1797)

The basic requirements for both assessment team leaders and members are the same. All team members should display a singular characteristic. They must have the ability to see the forest instead of the trees. They need to be able to see what is really happening. For many, this is a problem. There will be those who use the assessment as a platform to promote their individual, subjective agendas. These and other potential problems can be eliminated by

- Fostering teamwork as the way of doing things
- Involving the assessed organization as a partner
- Effective team leadership

Some problems can be avoided entirely. The eventual success of the effort is strongly related to its initial focus.

Initial Orientation

The team may decide to conduct an initial orientation to find out what's going on. Management by walking around is strongly endorsed. Walking around can provide real insight into ongoing activities. It can alert team members to real or potential deficiencies in operations. It can often (but shouldn't) come as a surprise that the customers and employees probably know more about what's really going on than supervisors or managers do. Ed Koch, the former mayor of New York, is an excellent example of someone who practiced this simple idea. His now famous question to anyone he met was "How am I doing?" Be willing to stop, look, and listen. There's an awful lot of good information out there just for the asking. How you ask is also important. Here are some suggestions.

1. Be objective. This would seem almost too obvious to mention. However, make sure inquiries do not appear subjective. If the interviewee senses an attempt to fix blame or other threat, no information will be given. Be sensitive to unspoken communication. Be impartial. Show empathy but not sympathy.

2. Seek answers. People rarely complain, even when asked. Make sure the information collection effort is not superficial. Don't coach or interpret. Take the time to listen actively. Start with a few, obvious questions, but allow latent issues to surface. Remember that concerns or complaints are lagging indicators of performance. Make a note to find out if these conditions still exist.

3. Experience perceptions. Recognize that people react to the entire environment. Look at the total picture. Remember

the adage of walking in someone else's shoes. Find out what people think about their job, how it might be done better, and so on. Psychologists classify job factors as satisfiers, neutral, or dissatisfiers. List these.

4.   Use innovative techniques. Avoid canned surveys or questionnaires. Start with a few key questions and let it go from there. Make some of these questions open-ended. Let interviewees define the key attributes or characteristics. You may get a surprise on this, something obvious you overlooked.

5.   Make sure you dig deep enough. The aim is to extract meaningful information. Follow any leads you suspect need further development. Recognize that articulation skills vary widely.

6.   Filter later. Don't believe everything you hear, but don't transmit this to the interviewee. Arguments are counterproductive and almost guaranteed to slow or halt any communications. Look for hidden agendas. Make sure you get enough valid information to justify dismissing the information later.

7.   Look for causal relationships. Quite often what is stated relates to other causes. This connection may not be apparent but must be eventually discovered. You don't want to throw away valuable data without checking thoroughly. Find out what the issue is all about first.

Other Means

The value of the initial orientation cannot be overemphasized. There are also other means of focusing any assessment effort. Determining exactly what is appropriate for a given organization in a particular situation is key to eventual success. Sometimes, it can be done using *not* logic. That is, it may be simpler to identify performance that is not all it could be. For example, assume an organization is experiencing a lot of unexpected problems. This suggests planning or implementation may not be adequate. If clear identification of problem areas or potential discrepancies are not provided by routine control measures, they are not adequate. If client/customer dissatisfaction does not directly correlate with the number and type of faults discovered, then the overall system is probably not effective. This logic may seem archaic and negative, given all that's been said so far. However, remember that we are looking for ways to focus improvement opportunities. The whole idea of a fault detection, reporting, and correction system is based on negatives. What we hope to achieve is an absence of negatives.

However, an absence of negatives does not always guarantee that everything is okay. It just doesn't work that way. An organization can easily be lulled by the artificial silence of a gagged system. This false sense of security can be created in a number of ways. One is that the system is not properly tuned. It does not look at the right things. Another is ineffective or biased analyses of reported deficiencies. Yet another is disregard. If the organization knew about the problem(s) all along, chances are the system is working okay. The organization simply chooses not to act on this knowledge. Doing nothing, postponing, or failing to correct or prevent the problem is a deliberate decision. This is unfortunate. Comprehensive and accurate assessments are performed, but the recommendations are ignored. In other cases, the results are unwittingly or deliberately altered so as to defeat their intended purpose.

How can this be prevented? First, recognize its probable cause. It is a culture problem. The real purpose of assessments needs to be understood by all members of the organization. The teamwork approach must be adopted. Individuals, groups, and organizations remain responsible for their own performance. To ensure their success, they must know and understand performance expectations. They must appreciate both their individual and collective role and purpose.

Planned and periodic assessments are a means to improve these activities. These assessments show how well the integrated effort is working. They identify any problems or conditions that hinder the individual, group, or organization from achieving its goals. They should be considered a win-win situation.

Selecting the Team

Selecting the Team Leader

The choice of the team leader is by far the most crucial ingredient for success in a performance-based assessment. His or her role most directly affects the planning, conduct, and acceptance of results. What are some of the needed characteristics? They include

- Strong leadership qualities. The team leader must be able to direct and control the assessment effort, provide a liaison with affected individuals, and maintain focus and schedule. All this needs to be done as a facilitator or catalyst, rather than a dictator.

- Objectivity. The team leader must ensure his or her and the team's total professionalism, ethical conduct, and objectivity. The ultimate success will hinge on this characteristic. There can be no hidden agendas or perception of subjectivity.

- Technical competence. Audit or surveillance training is helpful. An alternative is a basic understanding of the techniques of scientific inquiry. More importantly, a grasp of the issues is required. If the team leader is not an SME, he or she must at least be able to understand the importance of what is being analyzed. Credibility is an issue here.

- Team builder. The team leader must have demonstrated experience in this area. Without this, the assessment effort will produce results that are predictable.

- View toward improvement. Most compliance-oriented auditors cannot shed what will be viewed as bad habits. Finger pointing and fixing blame are not allowed. Once this perception exists, the whole effort is probably doomed. It is difficult to change. The aim is organizational improvement. Helping others, not "getting" them, should be the leader's goal.

Forming the Assessment Team

Team selection should be based on the type of assessment, activity or process, and the scope. Members of the team should be selected primarily on their expertise. Desired characteristics are similar to those listed for the team leader. Previous experience in performance-based assessments should be considered a plus. It may be the team makeup varies as the assessment proceeds through different stages. Remember the idea of a virtual team. Technical competence or operational experience will always be an issue. The team leader must recognize when additional help is needed. Team members share this responsibility and need to alert the leader when this occurs. Use consultants and outside technical experts if necessary.

Some of the most valuable team members will be those from the audited organization itself. Recognize there may be some turf concerns at first. These can be mitigated by the characteristics described earlier: objectivity, focus on improvement, and so on. Cultivate their input and participation.

Preparation and Training

Training for a performance-based assessment is totally different than for any other type. The traditional audit or surveillance training has already been described as helpful. It is not required. What is required is competency in the performance aspects of the process or activity. Team members who have been recruited for a particular expertise need to understand the application, if they do not already. Training related to the process or activity is therefore required. The real value lies in activity procedures, checklists, flow diagrams, and so forth.

Other preparation for the assessment would include identification of information sources, references, and so on. One of the more useful inputs is preliminary information gained from benchmarking studies. Some key questions are

- What are others doing? Are they better? If so, how and by how much?
- Why are they better? What's different? What's the same?
- What can we learn from them? Are there lessons here?

- How can we apply these lessons? Can we modify them to our situation?

Team selection—including the leader—training, and preparation are vital to eventual success. Time and care spent here will reap significant rewards. False starts should be expected. If the team consumes less than half the total assessment time redirecting the effort, it still will have beat the median or expected value. Don't be discouraged. It's the nature of the beast.

Overall Guidelines

In summary thus far, overall guidelines for the assessment team include:

- Establish clear intent for the assessment
- Define the scope along activity lines
- Ensure technical competence
- Foster a team approach
- Emphasize improvement
- Be professional and objective

Focused efforts with a well-defined scope have always been the hallmarks of an effective assessment (of any type). This is really nothing new. Administrative and scheduling considerations should encourage participation in the assessment efforts by the organization, group, or individual being evaluated. This is a little newer, but generally accepted practice. Joint assessment and goal setting is the foundation of management by objectives (MBO) and individual performance evaluations. Simply extend this successful idea.

Authority and responsibility need to be clearly understood. The role of the assessment team is to independently assess performance and identify potential improvements. It remains the responsibility of the affected individual, group, or organization to evaluate these recommendations and initiate any corrective or improvement actions. The end product is their property, not the team's.

Auditors *can* make recommendations. This is not new. It is consistent with all previous guidance. Unfortunately this option has not been exercised as often as perhaps it should have been. Technical experts, SMEs, and others have always been part of assessment efforts. Nothing new here either. What is new is the focus of performance-based assessments. For many organizations, this will require time for adjustment. Gradual acceptance will only come after successful demonstration of these techniques. However, the time allowed to make this adjustment is uncertain. The conclusion should be obvious. Start now. Start small if need be, but get going. Remember the saying,

> A journey of a thousand miles must begin with a single step.
> —The Way of Lao Tzu, Lao Tzu, sixth century B.C.

5

Designing
an Assessment Strategy

We dance round in a ring and suppose,
But the Secret sits in the middle and knows.
—Robert Frost, "The Secret Sits"

Effective planning is the key to eventual success. Preplanning efforts described in chapter 4 provide easy entry into this important phase. Experience suggests the complete lack of or less-than-adequate planning is the leading cause of organizational problems. Therefore the effort taken during designing (planning) an assessment strategy will provide significant return. There are two aspects to consider. First, the number of false starts is reduced. This happens when assessors get into the field study portion only to discover that the purpose and scope are not adequate. Perhaps more important, the real issues can be overlooked.

In addition to the purpose and scope, the assessment type and basis must be selected during this phase. The type of assessment (external, internal, or self) and basis (compliance, effectiveness, or performance) can also drastically influence the results and value of the effort. The purpose of the assessment will direct this selection. All of this is related to the expectations, particularly the benefits. This chapter will explore each of these issues in further detail.

Importance of the Planning Activity

Considerable guidance has already been provided on the formal techniques of planning audits and surveillances. These will not be repeated here. The planning steps discussed will focus on those aspects that specifically deal with the design of a strategy for effectiveness and performance-based assessments.

The minimum requirement for a performance-based assessment is direct observation of the process or activity. Planning should therefore aim toward that eventuality, suggesting the initial alignment. To understand the process or activity, construct rudimentary fishbone diagrams or flowcharts. This may seem an unnecessary effort, but later benefits will offset this preliminary work. Pulse points, those subactivities of particular interest or suspected problem areas because of the sequence or their impact should be selected. These aid the assessment team by flagging the more obvious places to look. Historical or trend information can be reviewed for clues. Above all, don't forget the initial orientation described in chapter 4. All these planning steps have one purpose: to get the effort off on the right foot.

Historical Information

Existing program, plant, or process descriptions, plans, or implementing procedures can reveal weaknesses and ambiguity. Obvious gaps can provide leads on where to look for performance problems or areas for improvement. Procedures, incidentally, are not limited to written documents. The term is used in the broader context. It refers to the repetitive or stylized fashion in which activities are performed. Quite often, this may be the lore of the ancestor or tribal knowledge. A particular way of doing things has been passed along. Be careful not to engage in self-fulfilling prophecies. It is tempting to jump at less-than-adequate or missing (formal) procedures as the apparent problem. Or to change the nature of the assessment to that of compliance based. Personnel may not be doing the right thing simply because they have not been told what the right thing is. Also, remember the new logic of performance-based assessments. Inadequate or missing procedures and failure to follow procedures are both cardinal sins in a compliance assessment. They may not negatively impact actual performance.

When conducting a review of previous performance history, it is sometimes useful to examine other indicators. Previous cautions on the real nature of certain performance indicators need restating. Examine all data critically. Some indicators or trends may be useful and should be looked at. For example, experience suggests that extensive retesting and rework may be opportunities for performance improvement. In service industries, these are activities that need to be done over again or checked. All these efforts are nonproductive. It is their very nature. Another check may be products that require constant replacement. This suggests the potential of inadequate preventive maintenance, design deficiencies, material problems, and so on. In design and manufacturing, indicators include the number (and type) of engineering changes, drawing or plan revisions, and material or component substitutions. Other miscellaneous indicators are project schedule slippages, employee turnover, the nature and number of customer complaints, accidents, and so on. Remember that the review of historical information is to point out areas in which there may be opportunities for performance improvement. The results are interesting clues but nothing more. All we've done so far is spot smoke. It will take looking into to find out if there is any fire.

Developing Lines of Inquiry

Planning for effectiveness and performance-based assessments is quite different from the detailed checklisting effort usually associated with compliance overviews. It is more accurately listing potential areas of interest (which may be revised or expanded upon) during the actual fieldwork. The document is often referred to as *lines of inquiry*. It consists of

1. The areas of interest based on preplanning and planning efforts
2. A preliminary list of the key attributes/ characteristics

Interviews with cognizant personnel in advance of the assessment are also helpful in developing this list. These interviews can provide honing of any issues listed during the review of historical information (and preliminary flow diagrams discussed later). They may also suggest areas or issues that should be included. The list should include any opening questions based on the initial orientation that were unanswerable. There may be residual issues based on interpretations of requirements or objectives.

Questions related to the formality of procedures may be included. The team will have to establish whether these are an obstacle to performance during the fieldwork. Remember that, in performance-based assessments, the activity may not be in accordance with any procedures but may still be proper and adequate. Objectivity is crucial in performance-based assessments. The signposts are not as clear as with compliance-based evaluations. This may cause consternation to some team members.

The outcome of the planning stage is an issues listing, not a formal checklist. It probably changed often during the historical review, activity or process analysis, and interviews. It will almost certainly change once the fieldwork commences. Its intended purpose is to serve as a guideline; to roughly focus the assessment. Performance-based assessments rely on direct, actual observation of the activity itself. The nature of this fieldwork is the principal feature distinguishing performance-based assessments from all other types.

Constructing Process Diagrams

Someone said a picture is worth a thousand words. The value of diagrams and charts is even greater when planning effectiveness and performance-based assessments. They are indispensable. One of the realities of TQM is that personnel skills will require sharpening. For example, assessors will need to understand (and be able to use) a wider variety of analytical tools. These include process capability studies, analysis of variance, sampling methods and analysis, flowcharting, Pareto analysis, and others. In the past, compliance auditors could read a procedure, formulate requirements into questions, and simply check on whether or not people were doing what they were supposed to. Not any more. Effectiveness and performance-based assessments leave this beaten path. They require a more disciplined, harder approach. For many, new skills will have to be acquired.

Fishbone Diagrams

Examples of graphic techniques that aid understanding of the process or activity are fishbone diagrams and flowcharts. These are not the only techniques available. However, they are presented to show their usefulness in planning effectiveness and performance-based assessments. The fishbone diagram is more accurately called an Ishikawa diagram, after its developer, Kaoru Ishikawa. It consists of a straight line which represents the process or activity. This line usually displays sequence from left to right. It can also represent time. Branches display major aspects or subactivities. The completed diagram, as the name suggests, looks like a fishbone. More accurately, it looks like a fish skeleton without the head. Further branching of these spines define subissues.

Two generalized fishbone diagrams are illustrated to demonstrate their construction. The first (Figure 5.1) is a fishbone diagram related to items, equipment, or a system (hardware). The major subcategories (spines) are design, manufacture, installation, operation, and maintenance. These are shown in their normal sequence. Further subissues along any given spine can be added to aid the analysis. For example, under design, subissues could include appropriate design criteria, design control, specification revision, and so on.

The same technique applies to any activity or process. For example, the fishbone diagram in Figure 5.2 might be constructed to analyze staffing of a project. As before, the main line (backbone) is the subject (personnel staffing). The major spines in this case represent components or aspects. The example lists several. They include definition of needs, selection/recruitment, training/education/experience, supervision, communications, procedures/methods, and control factors. Further branching along each spine can be added, if necessary.

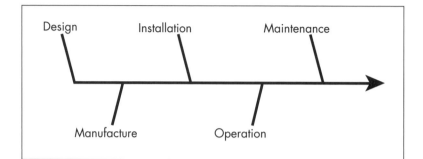

Figure 5.1
Generalized hardware fishbone diagram.

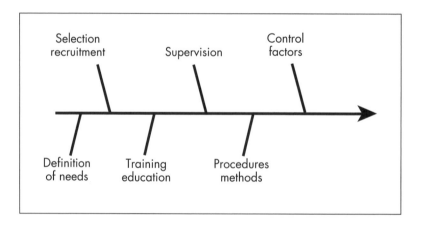

Figure 5.2
Generalized personnel staffing fishbone diagram.

Fishbone diagrams help develop comprehension of the components and subcomponents of any process or activity as well as their relationship. When completed, the diagram allows visualization. It aids spotting key areas and sequences.

Flowcharts

Another tool mentioned was the flowchart. Flowcharts come in several versions, but the basic technique is the same. As the name implies, flowcharts display the activity or process flow. Like fishbone diagrams, flowcharts are easy to construct. In the standard version, events or activities are shown as rectangles. Decisions are depicted as diamonds. Arrows are used to connect them to show sequence and relationship. Figure 2.1 is a simple example of this type of flow diagram.

More elaborate flowcharts show organizational involvement in the process or activity sequence. They are more time-consuming to construct, but clearly show exactly what is happening. An example of this type of flowchart is shown in Figure 5.3. It displays the processing of a customer order.

The flowchart shows an event-free situation. This is usually the easiest way to begin. The diagram is not finished, however. Note that there are pieces missing at each of the decision points. These must be filled in. It is not our intention to complete the entire diagram. One of these paths is shown to illustrate the further work needed. Figure 5.4 shows what happens when order entry runs into the situation that the item ordered is neither a standard or catalog item nor one that was previously quoted. The processing of the order normally proceeds no further until sales, engineering, and accounting departments provide some input.

Similar activities occur when item pricing or delivery commitments do not match standards. The completed flow diagram will show all these. Studying the completed diagram can reveal undesirable duplications, twists and turns, and missing pieces. The chart provides rapid, discernible understanding of a complex process.

Another version of flow diagrams is widely used for work simplification. The symbols used are shown in Figure 5.5 with an explanation of their meaning.

The same flow diagram shown in Figure 5.3 (processing a customer order) is depicted in Figure 5.6 using these symbols. The flowcharting technique is basically the same. One of the advantages of this system is that it clearly identifies toting, the movement of an item from one work area to another. Analysis of the diagram, supported by direct observations, will often result in these unproductive activities being eliminated or reduced. Another feature is that delays are shown.

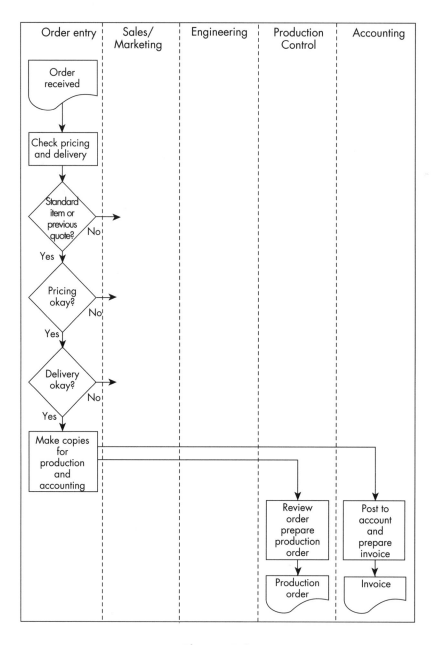

Figure 5.3
Flow diagram—customer order.

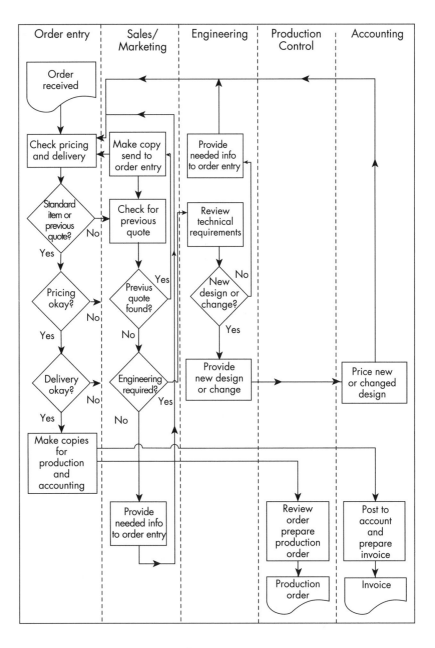

Figure 5.4
Flow diagram—customer order problems with item.

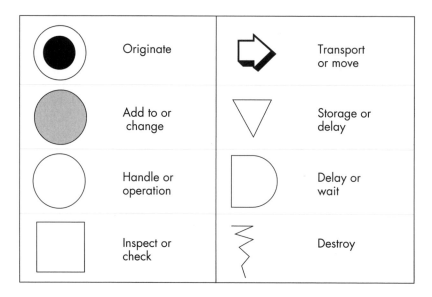

Figure 5.5
Work simplification symbols.

Note that there is not one operation that adds anything. The principal activities are verification, sorting, and routing. This type of flowchart, familiar to industrial engineers, is likewise useful for assessors. It is particularly valuable at the specific activity levels. Hint: These flowcharts and other worthwhile information (such as job descriptions) may already be on file somewhere in the organization. Look around for them. They may not be 100 percent accurate or up to date, but they will be a start.

Another example is an expansion of the systems diagram (shown in Figure 2.1) that is used by Lovelace Health Systems. This expanded diagram (see Figure 5.7) identifies specific activities important to providing the service(s) to the patient. Again, this example may prove helpful in other service industries.

Matrices

Matrices, as used herein, are not those familiar to mathematicians. They are tables, consisting of one or several rows and

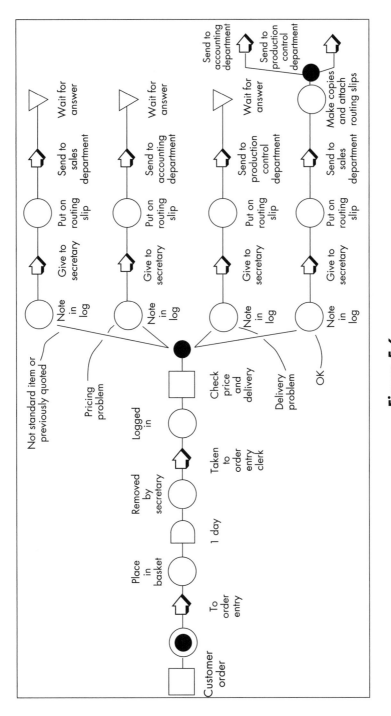

Figure 5.6
Flow diagram—customer order.

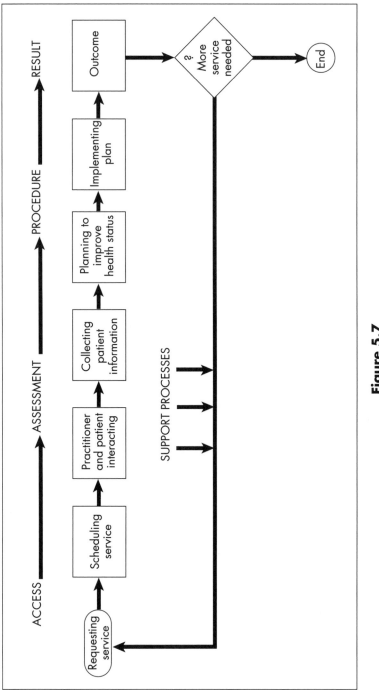

Figure 5.7
Flow diagram of health services at Lovelace Health Systems.

columns, constructed to display data or information as an aid in recognizing patterns and for other types of analysis. They can be used to show components and their significance. Significance can be defined by sequence, difficulty, cost, time, or other appropriate measure. Weighting will depend on the particular situation. An example of a matrix is shown in Figure 5.8. It uses the four categories most often used to define manufacturing processes: man, machine, material, and method. These can be, as the example shows, broken down into some of the more detailed issues to be examined during the assessment.

The matrix displays specific issues or potential improvements against each component or aspect. It can be used as a

Component	Issue	Line of Inquiry	Potential Improvement
Man	Poor bonding of endcaps to capacitor.	Observe swaging operation. Watch for proper temperature.	Thermostat on solder pot.
Machine	Solder iron tip wear.	See above. Check wattage of irons used.	Look into induction soldering techniques.
Material	Poor bonding of endcaps to capacitor.	Check proper solder is used. Are solder surfaces clean?	Look into possible fluxes. Check degreasing operation.
Method	See above.	Find out why different impregnants produce fewer problems.	This may be a materials issue or it may be that they're handled differently. In either case, substantially lower reject rate possible.

Figure 5.8
Matrix of components.

worksheet for the fieldwork. Once again, the matrix develops a baseline for understanding the process or activity characteristics. This in turn will result in effective planning.

Other matrices can be constructed using service factors or program goals. For example, the following aspects might be used to assess the performance of teachers.

- Competence in instructional techniques
- Interpersonal skills
- Planning and achieving standard educational goals
- Maintenance of professional skills
- Subject knowledge
- Peer/student/administration ratings

A matrix much like that shown in Figure 5.8 could be developed using these components.

Another version of a matrix is shown in Figure 5.9. In this matrix, preliminary analysis of intrinsic factors, source of variation, constraints, and influences is included. This matrix is constructed much like the previous one. However, further information regarding the process or activity is included. The characteristics are listed first. These may come from requirements, desired conditions, job-task analyses, process capability studies, or other sources. It then describes the type and amount of variation as well as its source next to each component. The matrix further describes any constraints. These may be system-imposed, personnel or equipment limitations, and so on. The last column lists any internal or external influences, potential or actual, that can affect the outcome.

Figure 5.9 shows only a portion of the design component in manufacturing. It shows that reliability requirements must be added to previous engineering standards. It demonstrates how the matrix can be used. Constructing this particular type of matrix admittedly takes more time. However, the thought processes involved in doing this focus on potential performance issues and possible improvements. The eventual matrix may still have some blanks come assessment time, but these can be filled in during the fieldwork.

Process	Intrinsic	Variation	Constraints	Influences
Design	Engineering standards	New reliability requirement	Current configuration Manufacturing capabilities Lack of life study data	Cost/profit Do not understand reliability concepts

Figure 5.9
Process or activity matrix.

Other Techniques

Other techniques useful during the planning phase to focus the assessment include

- PERT, critical path method, or other time-event networks
- Process control charts
- Pareto diagrams
- Job-task analyses
- Nominal group techniques
- Brainstorming

Any, several, or all of these techniques serve the same purpose: to help understand the process or activity which, in turn, will ensure meaningful planning.

Use of Performance Objectives

Performance objectives should be used when planning assessments. There can be problems, however. The first is that stated performance objectives are rarely found. The second is that, even when they are found, they are often not all they need to be. They may be flawed in terms of defining actual performance. Many are not quantifiable, making performance measurement difficult. For example, a hospital might state as a performance objective: "to reduce errors in laboratory test results." Using the objective as stated, any reduction, however insignificant, by definition meets this goal. If the time taken to analyze samples is increased and thereby reduces the potential error, is this better? Are there practical limits based on personnel training and experience or equipment capability? Does this performance objective include both routine and special tests? The point is that even when performance objectives are stated, the assessment team needs to examine them carefully. Proceeding further will require better definition.

If performance objectives are not stated, the team must devise them. They can be restatements of requirements related to performance. For example, the first cut at a performance objective might read: "Personnel shall receive adequate training to perform...(a particular activity)."

Since receiving training does not always directly relate to job skills and particularly performance, the objective might be rephrased as "Personnel will demonstrate the necessary skills and knowledge to perform...(the activity)."

This is closer to the mark. However, like the previous example of hospital tests, further definition is needed. The necessary skills and knowledge must be precisely listed. The devil is in the details. The assessment team must then either find a previous job-task analysis or construct one. The exact criteria that will be used to evaluate the performance objective must now be added. These criteria should include measures for their evaluation. Once again, process or activity knowledge will be essential. Let's assume one of the processes within the activity being evaluated involves welding. Because we have stated that personnel will demonstrate the necessary skills and knowledge to perform the particular activity, this includes the process of welding. This becomes one of the performance characteristics to be observed. As before, the statement "Perform a satisfactory weld" is grossly insufficient. Anyone familiar with welding can tell you there are a number of factors involved in producing a satisfactory weld. First, there are numerous welding techniques. Other factors include the base material itself, its thickness, the configuration of the weld, fit-up, preheat requirements, and so on. Our advantage, of course, is that we are looking at particular welds. Specifying the relevant characteristics will be easier. Remember also that, in performance-based assessments, we are limiting these to designate only the important or critical ones.

So we press on to come up with a list which more accurately defines what constitutes a satisfactory weld in this particular case.

For illustration, consider a very commonplace occurrence: changing a flat tire. There are many alternatives available when a flat tire occurs, however we will assume we wish to continue the journey. We will further add that we do not wish to drive further with the flat tire. The reason we have to state this is to eliminate this option. Someone will suggest "Why didn't you drive just around the corner to the gas station and let them fix it?" That would spoil our story.

Looking at the process simply, fixing a flat consists of the following activities.

1. Remove the jack and spare tire from the trunk.
2. Set the parking brake.
3. If possible, block the wheels.
4. Set the jack on level ground under the recommended lifting point.
5. Remove the hubcap and loosen the bolts on the flat tire.
6. Slowly jack up the wheel.
7. Remove the bolts and the flat tire.
8. Place the spare tire on the lugs.
9. Replace the bolts and tighten them.
10. Lower the car and remove the jack.

11. Place the flat tire and jack in the trunk.

12. Remove any blocks; release the parking brake.

We are now ready to continue our journey. In terms of this original performance objective, how many of these steps should be included in a list of critical or important activities? In selecting these, the key is in first accurately defining the task. For example, step 11 is more or less a housekeeping chore. Steps 2, 3, 4, and 12 relate to the safety of the operation. Steps 1 through 7 might be termed *set-up*. The actual replacement of the spare is covered in steps 8 and 9. Steps 10 through 12 are post-replacement activities. Step 5 might be considered important in terms of not stripping the threads or losing the nuts. Even in this simple example, the concept of analyzing a process and separating it into its component parts is helpful. Most processes or activities are very much like this. If you break them down into their sequence, you should be able to quickly discover those characteristics that are most important in terms of the stated performance objective. You could look at the rest, but you really don't have to.

Defining Valid Requirements

Much the same advice is offered here. It is not unusual to find a plethora of requirements listed for a particular process or activity. Many of these apply only partially (although this is not always clearly stated). Others were listed because someone (you can never find out exactly who) somehow thought them appropriate. The harder work of lifting the appropriate requirements from these standards was never done. Perhaps it was assumed that either users or auditors have the knowledge and time to do so. Or maybe, someone was just being conservative, playing it safe. The result is that many activities or processes are unduly (and expensively) constrained by full compliance to broad standards when this is not really necessary. However, when the assessment is based on effectiveness or performance, comments regarding the validity of any and all requirements are allowed, even encouraged. Look at what is happening and what is needed. Then look at the list of requirements. Put a check next to those that apply. Recommend the others be evaluated. Drop them if you don't need them. Why carry this unnecessary burden?

You might also find that many valid requirements are not listed. The reasons for this are legion. Standards are constantly updated, replaced, or added. Laws are introduced or changed. For example, there are probably still some firms unaware of environmental protection requirements that apply to their activities. In defining valid requirements, it may be necessary to add some that were not there before.

As with performance objectives, sufficient detail must be provided for a meaningful assessment. Some codes and standards are notoriously vague. After all, they were written to apply to almost all situations. Yours may not be like that at all. In other cases, only certain parts of the code or standard apply. Reduce it down to the specifics. Otherwise, it is like painting on the head of a pin with a 4-inch brush.

Performance-based assessments offer the opportunity for factual performance measurement and identification of needed improvements. Providing a valid list of requirements is one of these.

Situational Analysis

Performance is often highly related to the specific situation and surrounding circumstances. The level of performance is definitely influenced by the individual's perception of these factors. Athletes respond to the Olympic challenge, musicians to an appearance at Carnegie Hall. Actors refer to the performance of their entire career. At the other end of the spectrum, routine, day-to-day, largely unobserved performances seldom cause mildly elevated adrenalin levels. In fact, they may be quite mechanical and unthinking.

This observation leads to another interesting way to analyze performance in terms of situation and importance. We can borrow some concepts from statistics used in analyzing stocks, for example, and from economics, in explaining total costs. This is called *regression analysis;* readers unfamiliar with these techniques can find further information in any number of statistical or economic textbooks.

The equation of a straight line is as follows:

$$y = bx + a$$

where y is the value to be predicted (dependent variable), x is the independent variable, b is the slope of the line (which describes the relationship between the two), and a is a fixed value (constant).

This has been used in stocks, for instance, where the slope is used to describe how a particular stock or mutual fund moves.

In economics, total cost is considered the sum of the fixed and variable costs. The slope represents variable costs per unit, the fixed cost is a constant. The total cost (y) is equal to fixed and variable costs in accordance with the previous formula, based on the number of units (x).

To utilize the same concept in terms of performance, a horizontal (x) scale could be constructed representing the degree of challenge or difficulty represented by situational factors. The vertical (y) scale represents performance level. This is shown in Figure 5.10.

The a value represents the fixed, constant, base level performance (normal routine). The situational response is shown by the slope. Depending upon the particular circumstances, analysis of this model can be enlightening. If the required performance level under extreme circumstances cannot be achieved, there may be problems. An example might be an airline pilot in an emergency situation. While not routine, overall performance must be sufficient to ensure satisfactory responses (performance) at this extreme.

Overall performance can also be improved by raising the base level. Base level expectations can be raised. In certain situations, increases in normal (expected) performance may be attainable. Thinking in this fashion, that is, separating performance within normal operations and in specific situations may aid in planning and assessing both the expected and stretch levels. As you might expect, this is highly dependent on the particular activities.

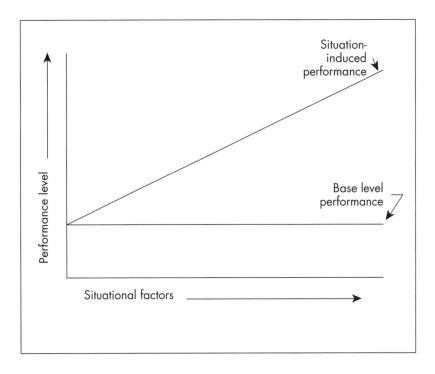

Figure 5.10
Performance versus situational factors.

Guidance for Selecting the Assessment Approach

An accurate depiction of the process or activity will aid in developing a preliminary listing of the issues of interest. The next step is the selection of an assessment approach. Remember that there are three basic types of assessments: internal, external, and self. These assessments may be based on compliance, effectiveness, or performance. Refer again to Figure 3.2. Each of these combinations has particular merit, depending upon the circumstances. Remember that the basic types of assessments are largely dependent on perspective. The basis depends on the focus. From a results standpoint, the most desirable type is self-assessment. Next best is internal. However, the nature of the issues may be at cross purposes. For example, a self-assessment related to compliance may not produce results unless the need for this comes externally. Otherwise, the individual or group will make the same assumptions regarding compliance it already has. Selecting the best assessment strategy (both type and basis) therefore requires some thinking in advance. There's a bright note, though. You can always change strategy during the assessment itself, if this seems warranted. For example, if issues arising during the assessment seem less appropriate to compliance or effectiveness, then performance aspects might be added. If the organizational resources do not seem adequate to identify or resolve these issues, external input can be obtained. All of this may seem confusing to the typical compliance auditor. After all, a plan is a plan. Under the newer rules for conducting assessments, we agree. However, we add that a plan can be changed. It is just a plan, a starting point. Results are more important than how well the plan was followed.

Returning again to the initial selection of assessment strategy, answers to two basic questions will help identify the best approach. The first is: What is the purpose of the assessment? While this may sound too simplistic, assessments should have some purpose. If the purpose is to verify compliance with requirements, proceed to the choice of type. Once again, the best type is self-assessment provided all requirements are clearly identified and the individual, group, or organization is aware of them. On the other hand, to demonstrate compliance to others, then the better type of assessment might be external. An example of this would be the review of corporate books by certified public accountant (CPA) firms usually presented in annual reports. The characteristic of independence is important.

When there are concerns about system operation or effectivity, then the effectiveness basis is more appropriate. The more logical types may be either internal or external assessments. In this case, perspective is important. Perhaps a fresh viewpoint is, too. When a group within an organization enlists the aid of another, while the assessment is internal as regards the organization, it is external to that particular group.

The benefits (and drawbacks) to internal versus external assessments are similar to those listed for internal versus external boards of directors. There are pros and cons to both approaches. There is some advantage to a fresh look, a different perspective. Many elegant solutions to issues or problems have been borrowed from unrelated areas. At other times, it may stem from the (most times unwittingly) nearsighted fashion of the problem statement. Consider the difference had Thomas Edison set out to develop a better candle. Making the deposit slip easier to fill out is very different than (the broader) making deposits easier.

Choosing the basis is also easy. Performance-based assessment concepts and techniques are perhaps most easily understood by contrasting them with traditional compliance-based activities. Some of the more significant and fundamental differences between performance-based and compliance-based overview activities follow. The performance-based approach to assessments

- Requires direct observation of activities (compared with review of documentation or compliance to procedures)

- Focuses on processes or activities most directly impacting operations, safety, reliability, or maintainability (as compared to either a systematic or random selection of all activities)

- Includes an evaluation of not only whether, but to what extent, product or service goals are being achieved or not (as compared to focusing on identifying noncompliances with procedures/requirements)

- Requires technical expertise or knowledge of operations to evaluate the selected component/system, activity, or program

- Adds the step in which the significance of any recommendation or finding is analyzed and documented (compared to letting the statement of noncompliance stand silent relative to its importance)

- Adds the process whereby the underlying or apparent cause(s) of less-than-adequate performance is analyzed

Two of the important concepts during this evaluation stage are the graded approach and root cause analysis. Adoption of a graded approach will greatly influence selecting the assessment type. The graded approach suggests that the assessment effort fits the situation and its importance. It is predicated on these two factors. The graded approach implies the appropriate amount and rigor of the assessment consistent with its impact or consequence on the organization. This means that, among other criteria, the depth, scope, and focus of any assessment will be influenced by its importance to the organization. Performance-based assessments are unnecessary for relatively straightforward activities with minimum operational impact. Save them for the class of issues that can be called *showstoppers*. Find out about and fix the things that are really wrong first; return to those of lesser importance later.

Identifying Opportunities for Improvement

Of the strategies discussed, performance-based assessments offer the best opportunity to improve operations or activities. During the planning stages, potential opportunities for improvement should be identified. This may be revised during the actual conduct and analysis phases of the assessment. Hopefully this list will be expanded. After all, this is the payback for the extra effort involved.

How do you identify opportunities for improvement? Many come by carefully examining whatever diagnostics were used during the preplanning stage. Possible reductions in paper flow, streamlining of activities, introduction of more error-free methods, and other performance improvement possibilities are suggested in this fashion. Look at Figures 5.3, 5.4, and 5.6. Can you spot any opportunities for improvement?

Opportunities for improvement can be identified negatively. Issues and surfaced problems identified during the historical review or trend analysis need solution. Interviews with affected personnel may have also provided some leads. Effective benchmarking will likewise yield candidates.

Opportunities for improvement include, but are not limited to

- Faster, easier ways to do the same thing
- Ways to do them better
- Ways to increase effectiveness
- Productivity or efficiency increases
- Removing obstacles to performance
- Reducing the potential for problems or errors
- Promoting excellence

Performance-based assessments should proceed no further unless at least one hoped-for positive outcome is identified. Effectiveness or performance-based assessments must have some minimal purpose. Otherwise, the effort is reduced to one of stumbling around, offering to help, but mostly getting in the way. In terms associated with aimless compliance assessments, it is nothing more than a fishing trip.

Evaluation of Benefits

Performance-based assessments are significantly different from traditional compliance-based audits or surveillances. These differences force several changes in methodology. Performed properly, a performance-based assessment requires considerably more effort. The truth is that it will require

- More time
- More detailed planning
- More attention to team staffing
- More flexibility
- More analysis and framing of recommendations
- More care with the final report
- Increased attention during the corrective/preventive action and closeout phase

However, the results can more than offset the investment. Improvements to activities and operations can result in tremendous payback to the organization. Their essence is results, not form or format. They are more likely to effect movement, more quickly, on any identified deficiencies. Interviews with auditees reveal that they consider the resulting performance-based reports more useful. They are more motivated to get involved with the program or install needed improvements. Much of this is the result of the creation of a team approach before, during, and after the assessment itself. Follow the advice given just previously. Do not undertake an effectiveness or performance assessment without some preliminary expectation. Be able to articulate at least one hoped-for improvement. Ensure that the assessed organization clearly understands this purpose, scope, and intent. Encourage everyone's full participation. When the overall tone has been proactive, positive, focused on improvement, and participative, these results should not be surprising. Remember that when benefits are listed, they should be the customers'. In most assessments, the customer is the assessed individual, group, or organization.

Potential benefits (opportunities for improvement) were characterized previously. It was pointed out that the assessment planning should include one or several of these expected outcomes. As has been the usual advice, these expected benefits should be quantified. Effective planning will allow an expected result to be stated (for example, that order processing time be reduced by at least 10 percent). It may be worthwhile to set stretch goals at this point as well. These represent improvements that seem possible at the outset. Perhaps in our example of order processing, the team feels that by eliminating duplications and performing activities in parallel rather than in series, an overall reduction of 50 percent is possible. This will only be supported by the assessment and later analysis, of course. But it's a distinct possibility. State both the expected and stretch goals. Aim high. By doing this, you have already set an extremely positive tone for the assessment effort.

6

Focusing on the Issues

Facts are stubborn things.
—Alain Rene Le Sage, Gil Blas, bk. X, 1

This chapter talks about focusing on the real issues. This is one of the promised benefits of effectiveness or performance-based assessments. They are supposed to provide a critical, knowledgeable look at processes and activities. This evaluation is more than compliance to standards; it is accurate measurement of performance and improvement. The intent is to objectively scrutinize what's really happening. After looking carefully, improvements can then be identified. However, it is easy to get distracted. Things are often not what they appear to be. Problems are not caused by what we sometimes think they were. The ultimate success of the effort will be judged by a simple criterion: Did we find some way to do things better? To identify obstacles to improvement, we need to go beyond symptoms or apparent causes, and get to the real, more basic issues. We need to be like Sergeant Joe Friday: "Just the facts, ma'am."

Finding the Real Problems—Distinguishing Among Symptoms, Apparent Causes, and Root Causes

Performance can be highly subjective. Defining its aspects can also depend on a number of factors. Measuring performance characteristics is difficult unless quantifiable criteria have been established during the planning stage. It is particularly hard to do when people or values are involved.

We are a remarkably diverse lot. Motivation varies considerably among individuals, both in strength and source. Many years ago, the behavior of workers was described in terms of Theory X and Theory Y. Theory X held that individuals were basically lazy, did not like to work, had to be driven and closely watched to get any results at all. Theory Y held the opposite. Neither extreme held up well. Others added Theory Z, sort of a middle path. Theory Z talked more about the system and its impact on individuals. These theories have been largely discarded. In any group of individuals, there are perhaps only a few on either end of this X-Y axis. Most fall somewhere in between. Theory Z did have one embedded truth. In most (80 percent or more) of the cases of less-than-adequate performance or failure to improve, the system is at fault. It does impact the individual.

This should not force the general conclusion that the system is almost always at fault or needs changing. We have alluded to the importance of corporate culture and stressed the importance of a no-fault environment for improvement to occur. We have also emphasized teamwork and collaboration as an effective means to ensure a successful outcome. Performance can be individual or collective, but it always is played against some background. With organisms as complex as we are, there are myriad factors at work. Some are obvious, many are not. The assessor must screen all of this information to obtain a meaningful evaluation. Like the early gold prospectors, we may pan a lot of sand before we find what we're looking for.

Distinguishing Symptoms from Causes

Assessors need to be able to distinguish symptoms from causes. Symptoms are the tangible evidence or manifestation(s) that something is wrong. In medicine, symptoms like fever and muscle ache result from disease or infection. These symptoms are not the cause. The disease or infection is. Symptoms merely provide visible, often measurable indication. For example, a fever can be detected with a thermometer, although this does not identify the cause.

Symptoms are what are most often observed during an assessment. Excessive absenteeism is a symptom. So is failure to take responsibility. There are many others. All we have so far is sand. More sifting is needed.

Getting to the Causes

To finally get to the real issues, we must go further than identifying symptoms. Once again, there are different kinds of causes. Some are direct, others indirect. Some are contributory, others are apparent. Apparent causes are the immediate or conspicuous reasons for an issue or problem. Upon further investigation, excessive absenteeism may be attributed to lax supervision, recent work rule changes, or some other reason. These are the first reasons beyond the symptoms. One or several may even be the *real* reason. It could also be one that underlies these or has not even been mentioned yet. This is the root cause, the real and most basic reason.

All too often, causes assigned by those directly involved with or who observe or relate an event or occurrence are not totally reliable. For example, consider interviewing witnesses to an accident. Testimony is often clouded by emotions and confusion. Trained investigators recognize this. Although eyewitness information is valuable, it does not serve as the sole basis for the investigation. It is normally separated into its components and used with other data. Only the resultant facts are used.

Maintaining discrimination between reality and perception is significant. If only symptoms or apparent causes are considered, then improvement is not likely to happen.

Concepts of Root Cause

The *root cause,* as the name suggests, is that most basic reason a problem, less-than-adequate performance, or obstacle to improvement exists. Root cause analysis encompasses a variety of techniques, both informal and structured, used to determine these reasons. Root cause analysis techniques are most often used in the reactive mode, that is, to uncover the reason for existing deficiencies. However, these same techniques can be used in the prospective (forward-looking) mode to anticipate and thereby avoid future problems. Root causes of performance barriers must be clearly identified and properly corrected, before any real improvement can be expected. When planning changes, these root causes must be eliminated before they reinfect the new system.

The use of root cause analysis techniques in effectiveness or performance-based assessments cannot be overemphasized. Since the focus is on results, the analysis of results must likewise provide meaningful, accurate direction. Root cause analysis provides objective, not subjective conclusions. After all the planning, careful observations, rechecking of information, and other facets of a properly performed assessment, the results certainly deserve an effective analysis.

Effective Problem Solving

Root cause analysis techniques have also been described as basic problem-solving tools. Problem solving is effective when issues do not recur or spread. Problems are everyone's responsibility, even if they appear to surface in one area. Even apparently trivial problems can affect the overall operation and result in inefficiencies and customer dissatisfaction. Trivial problems often combine or grow to become major problems. Effective problem solving ensures that issues are correctly tagged. Production problems might be traced to design oversights or the failure to allow for manufacturing or material variations. The design itself might be modified to reduce or eliminate the problem. Teamwork and sharing of responsibility are essential to any real progress toward problem elimination and the improvement of overall performance.

Effective problem solving is a higher level skill. It requires knowledge, ability, and experience. It involves the application of tools or techniques. Training and practice will enhance competency. These tools include statistical process control (SPC), analysis of variance, design of experiments, trend analysis, process capability studies, Pareto analysis, and others. Numerous surveys reveal the most desirable employee skill is problem solving. Skills identified as important for supervisory and management personnel, also rank problem solving after communicating management commitment and defining customer requirements.

Typical Systemic or Generic Problems

The following list of typical systemic issues is provided for reference. They represent some of the more common, generic problems that may be encountered. They are useful to the assessor as convenient buckets to classify observations.

1. Work practices. Methods or procedures (both written and unwritten) used in the routine performance of a task or activity. These include any necessary preparation, the use of documents, equipment or material, and practices for error detection.

2. Training/qualification. Proficiency in the task or activity. This includes any specified qualification/certification, training (formal or informal), and its effectiveness.

3. Work organization/planning. Scoping, planning, organizing, and scheduling the performance of a task or activity.

4. Communications. The transfer of information, whether spoken or written. Effectiveness can be judged by both content and method.

5. Supervision. Techniques used in directing and monitoring personnel in the performance of their assigned task or activity.

6. Management methods. Techniques used to provide organization, program and administrative policies, overall resource and schedule planning, direction of activities, interface with other organizations, and control and oversight of activities.

Note: The following two categories are really part of management methods, but are listed separately to be able to discriminate between them later, if need be.

7. Resource allocation. Allocating labor, material, or other resources, including financial, to accomplish a particular task/objective. Effectiveness is judged by schedule and priority decisions.

8. Change management. The process of modifying/revising a particular process or operation. This includes both hardware and software (such as procedures, organization, document revision, and so on) as well as transition planning.

9. Physical conditions. Physical and environmental conditions, equipment layout, accessibility, and other factors in the work area that impact personnel or equipment performance.

10. Man/machine interface. The design and maintenance of equipment/items used to communicate information to personnel (tags, labels, signs, alarms, and so on) or from personnel (controls) that impact plant/system performance.

11. Design. The design and configuration of equipment/systems (or subsystems). This includes initial design bases and the control of any required modifications or changes.

12. Procurement. The process of acquiring necessary resources, personnel, equipment, material, or systems.

13. Equipment manufacture and installation. Includes on- or off-site manufacturing/assembly of equipment, storage, and handling, up to and including its initial installation.

14. Plant/system operation. The actual operation of permanently installed, temporary, or portable equipment or systems in their intended function.

15. Maintenance/testing. Management system and process of maintaining equipment, processes, or systems in optimum condition. Includes preventive maintenance, calibration, and repairs.

16. Documentation. Preparation, approval, completion, distribution, control, and retention of appropriate instructions, procedures, drawings, and other documentation or records of activities.

17. External. Influence outside the usual control of the organization. Includes requirements imposed by other agencies or organizations, weather, sabotage, and so on.

Use of these categories during the assessment will aid in focusing the specific issues more quickly. This list can be modified as necessary.

The basic statistics student is taught that, when grouping data, the optimal number of classes is between seven and 16. Below seven, the categories become so large that patterns are lost; above 16, there are too many to show the grouping. When examining issues, it is useful to have categories similar to the ones listed here. They are also functional during the analysis phase. It's fascinating to watch certain patterns emerge as the assessment proceeds.

Involving the Customer

The customer of the assessment effort is the individual, group, or organization being assessed. Their involvement in the effort should have begun in the preliminary planning stages. They should have helped identify and shape the expected improvement goals. To the extent practicable, they should participate in the assessment itself. They will certainly want to be part of the later analysis and framing of corrective, adaptive, preventive, and performance improvement strategies.

This will require revision of the working practices of formal compliance auditors. It will also require learning on the auditee's part. In the previous adversarial environment, trust was not characteristic. In the newer culture, both stretch and expected improvement goals are sought. Reaching these goals brings credit to the assessor and the customer alike.

Transition to this pleasing state of affairs may take time. Remember our old nemesis, corporate inertia. Getting there is sometimes best accomplished by a series of smaller wins rather than hoping for one large victory. Start with manageable pieces. Use evolution rather than revolution. Success breeds success. Find those areas that everybody thinks need fixing. First, you have built-in support. You also have a predisposition to change. It might be something as simple as time reporting or the issuing of material to the assembly line. It could be the

way in which project status is reported. The point is to find
something doable, reasonably straightforward, which also represents a tangible opportunity for improvement. Once again,
the customer can probably give you quite a list of these. All
you need to do is ask. Start with a simple question like: "What's
in the way of your doing a better job?"

Customer Surveys

Much has been written on conducting customer surveys; some
of it is worthwhile, some not. One of the most important traps
to avoid is the self-fulfilling prophesy. For example, consider
the question: "What do you like best about our bank?" What's
the hidden assumption? Another problem is the survey mode.
A telephone survey of voters, conducted many years ago, predicted the exact opposite outcome in a presidential election. It
was recognized later that, at that time, only those with above-
average income had telephones. Think about the last product
survey you responded to. Were the questions phrased to produce a specific outcome?

Scientists refer to these problems as the error of the instru-
ment. Even our little question "What's in the way of your doing
a better job?" has embedded assumptions. First, that there's
something in the way and second, that the person could do his
or her job better were these removed. In fact, with the wrong
tone, the question could sound like an accusation of less-than-
adequate performance. The trick is to minimize these flaws.
Accept that the questions can probably never be perfect. Just
try to make them as good as possible.

Here are some of the other traps to avoid.

- Assuming you know what the customer wants. This
  trap may not be deliberately stepped into. It may spring
  from an honest belief supported by reason of knowledge, experience, and hidden facts.

- Asking the wrong questions. Already alluded to
  previously, this also includes questions so vague or
  generic that they yield no useful, specific information.

- Asking questions that have no measurement. Some
  questions by their nature are qualitative. In these cases,

be sure to have some sort of scale in mind to ensure meaningful data later.

- Poorly constructed scales. People think in a linear fashion. When people are asked to rate something on a scale of one to five, they normally think a straight line. This is a problem with employee evaluations. While the written instructions might be clear, the application of the values is not. If the instructions state that the four to five rating represents exceptional performance, with only 5 percent of the people you know being in this range, the picture is more like Figure 6.1b than 6.1a.

- Cause-and-effect relationships. The link between customer expectations and behavior needs to be clearly established. Needs should be separated from wants.

- Failure to develop a situation-specific survey. The survey should be targeted to the situation at hand. Do not attempt global solutions for a minor problem or issue. Avoid questions that deal with the meaning of life or the creation of the universe. Use the right terminology in the questions. Build the survey around the particular situation and its importance.

Once you're sure you've asked the right questions, listen carefully to the answers. If need be, think of your customer as the ghost of Christmas future. Unless you change your (individual, group, or corporate) ways, the vision may be bleak.

Customer Involvement in the Assessment Effort

The customer should also participate in the assessment efforts. If the tone set has been positive and collaborative, this will not be a problem. It may be just the opposite, because it is the customers' particular activities that will be improved. They are motivated. There is really no benefit to covering up. Likewise, their input to the analysis virtually guarantees their acceptance of the results. After all, these are their ideas.

Performance assessments require direct observation of the process or activity. It might be argued that, if customers participating in the assessment effort are also under observation, there will be bias introduced. This possibility obviously exists.

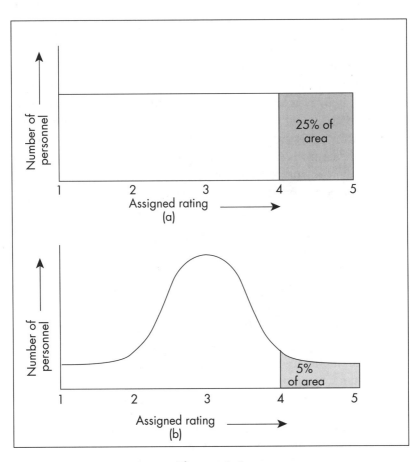

Figure 6.1
Linear versus nonlinear rating scales.

This is usually countered by the team effort involved. If a positive, no-fault attitude exists, this undesirable influence can be lessened. In truth, when properly conducted, every assessment will be more or less a self-assessment. The team leader's role is more a referee, catalyst, and trainer than anything else. The assessment takes on a momentum all its own. This reinforces the previous importance given the selection of the team leader and members. It also emphasizes the need for proper planning and the identification of improvement opportunities prior to the assessment effort getting underway.

Forming Sound Conclusions

Sound conclusions resulting from the assessment are the crown jewels of the effort. They should flow logically from the planned goals and later fieldwork. They should line up as shown in Figure 6.2.

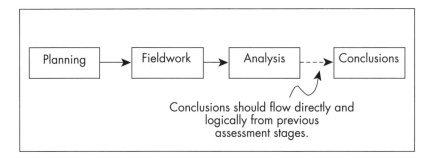

Figure 6.2
Lining up the plan and conclusions.

Another way of looking at this is to state them in sequence. See if it makes sense when you say it out loud.

- The purpose of the assessment was…(fill in goal).
- Observations revealed…(fill in results).
- Our conclusion is therefore…(fill in inference).

If the advice given thus far is followed, the customer should agree with these conclusions. Needless to say, the final recommendations for improvement will be based on these conclusions. Let us add some cautions, however.

Testimony Versus Evidence

Compliance auditors have a relatively straightforward task. Given stated requirements, they need only verify compliance. Effectiveness or performance-based assessors may stray far from this beaten path. In doing so, they can easily fall into the testimony versus evidence trap.

Testimony, as the name infers, refers to statements obtained during the fieldwork and interviews. These may be very useful for any number of purposes. One obvious use is in refining or narrowing issues. Another is in developing new lines of inquiry. However, like testimony in court, it can be refuted or dismissed. Some of it represents unsupported opinions. As such, they can be challenged.

Before the fieldwork is completed, testimony that will be used must be supported by evidence. The firmer this support, the better. Facts must be obtained and quantified to the extent necessary to frame the issue. For example, if an interviewee states that perhaps up to one-third of all rework may not be recorded, the team must attempt to flesh out this statement. This may be accomplished by examining time sheets, observing the actual rework, or finding other evidence. The original allegation must be supported by tangible facts.

Validation for compliance purposes would consist only of enough instances of undocumented rework to firm up the finding. In effectiveness or performance-based assessments, the investigation must proceed much further. The issue must contain some evaluation of its cause and consequences. So the team must look for the circumstances. The consequences of a significant amount of rework being performed but not being recorded should be obvious. The reasons (if true) are of even more interest. These may range from underlying basic design, materials or manufacturability, supervision, or personnel training inadequacies to seemingly unrelated, often bizarre reasons. This is another example of the need for experience and process/activity knowledge on the part of the team members.

Most companies do not really know the amount of rework they routinely perform. Recent studies have shown U.S. firms incur approximately 20 percent in rework costs. This is a tremendous competitive disadvantage. It is particularly sobering, because it means that, out of five workers, one spends full time fixing mistakes the others make. Incidentally, rework includes redoing calculations that are wrong, rewriting procedures that are inadequate, and reteaching a class the same material. Just because your firm is not in manufacturing or construction, do not assume rework does not apply to you.

Sampling and Risk Avoidance

To date, formal compliance audits have been subjective as regards sampling. The number of items checked during the audit to verify compliance (or not) was the choice of the auditor. Little attention was given to statistical significance when presenting the results.

The graded approach suggests that scrutiny given an item, process, or activity depend on its importance. Sizable inaccuracies in the results can be introduced by sampling error. Sampling error is directly related to the size of the sample taken. Obviously, the number of observations made should be proportional to the importance of the activity or process. Figure 6.3 shows the number of observations required to achieve 95 percent confidence in the process effectiveness statement, given *no* unsatisfactory findings. (This is loosely stated: Statisticians prefer a 5 percent Type II error probability in testing the hypothesis that the process is the stated value of effectiveness or better).

Process Effectiveness	Sample Size
95%	58
90%	28
85%	18
80%	13

Figure 6.3
Sample size versus process effectiveness.

The table in Figure 6.3 was derived using the binomial distribution, which assumes an equal chance of observing unsatisfactory performance during each observation ($p = 0.5$). There are also formulae to determine sample size given an expected percentage in the population and allowable error. These are used extensively for opinion polls. Statistical competence will be one of the hallmarks of the new age assessor. Teams must either have at least one member reasonably comfortable with statistical inference and risk assessment or have access to this expertise. When the purpose of the assessment is important enough, there is no practical reason not to have accurate results.

Evaluating Risk or Importance

This should have been done during the planning stage. If new facts have emerged during the fieldwork, the risk or importance of the assessed process or activity must be reevaluated. There are many techniques available to perform this analysis. It can also be done on a semiformal basis using criteria developed by the team and customer.

For performance-based assessments, this analysis needs to extend down to the specific activity level. What a bank teller does when there are no customers might be an effectiveness issue. What the teller does during a customer transaction relates to performance. In evaluating importance, concentrate on the job aspects thought important. Too many assessments get derailed by focusing on criteria that are irrelevant to the issue.

Cost and Schedule Considerations

Most recommendations are constrained by cost or effectiveness considerations. Conclusions should not be. They should be statements of fact supported by the assessment effort.

The effects of constraints in formulating recommendations is discussed in detail in chapter 7 of this book. The point in mentioning constraints, such as cost or effectiveness, is to emphasize their role in the overall process. They factor in later. The conclusions should accurately paint the picture. How and when the needed improvements can be made is a separate issue. Do not allow them to be an influence at this stage of the effort, whether consciously or not.

Peer Review

Peer reviews should be sought. It is easy to lose focus and subjectivity when staring at any issue long enough. The trick is to find others with sufficient knowledge or understanding of the issues and the requisite objectivity. This is one situation in which external help may be needed. Taking this option requires that the reviewer also understand the assessment goals. Internal reviews should be continuously performed. Bouncing issues and formative conclusions off another team member who has not been involved in that particular area can sometimes be helpful. Customer managers may be good candidates for peer reviews.

Decision accuracy is at stake here. Check your results. Ask others to verify them. What you're doing is important. Get all the input you can.

Field Activities

Fieldwork for an effectiveness or performance-based assessment takes more time and work than for one based on compliance. Additional time is needed for the detailed observations that form the basis for these techniques. We have already pointed out that the planning effort is also significantly greater (or should be).

During the fieldwork in an effectiveness or performance-based assessment, the question will arise as to how far to go in tracing an identified problem or issue. There are two rules to follow here.

1. Determine the significance of the problem or issue. If it is significant, follow the trail of evidence to the last apparent cause that can be identified. Refer to rule 2 for further guidance. It is recommended that, when a serious issue surfaces, available time and resources be spent determining the real cause rather than searching for additional examples of the same problem.

2. Gather sufficient information to allow an effective root cause analysis to be performed later. We understand this implies some understanding of these techniques to follow this rule, however, this particular need has already been suggested. Some expertise must either be team-resident or

available during the planning and fieldwork to guide this information gathering effort.

Following this advice may result in a tradeoff of the planned scope, unless unlimited time and resources are available. It may result in violating the sampling requirements described previously to come up with a defensible conclusion. It may be necessary to defer some of the planned activities for a later assessment. When this category of issue surfaces, it is time for a war council by the team. Following this advice does not, however, violate the basic concepts of effectiveness and performance-based assessments. Remember the primary focus should be on characteristics important in the particular situation. You've found one or several. Forget any lesser issues. Concentrate on the significant ones you have found.

Looking at Self Checks

One of the important activities undertaken during the fieldwork is the examination of self checks which are part of work practices previously mentioned. Evaluating their effectiveness is a fundamental part of analyzing performance. It should be pointed out that many of these checks are not formally prescribed. There are many instances in which performance self checks are equally or more effective than any elaborate quality assurance program. The best example is the story of the upside-down part. The authors have heard this story in many versions. Its veracity may be doubtful, but it goes something like this. A company noticed that, all of a sudden, assemblies were coming off the line with one part installed upside down. The drawings, when checked, sure enough, showed the part in this wrong orientation. But the drawings were old. The assembly had been produced for many years with no problems. Puzzled, the engineers looked further and finally noticed that the problems occurred soon after a particular worker had retired. Pursuing this lead, they interviewed the retired worker. He calmly stated that, yes, he knew the drawings were in error. As he placed the part on the assembly, he had been putting it on the right way. When he retired, his replacement had conscientiously followed the drawings.

There are many instances of these local fixes to known deficiencies. Many are undocumented. The drawing never got changed in our little story. It might be argued that performance was not an issue (during the time the worker made the needed correction), but replication was a problem. The assessor must diligently observe what is going on. Sometimes following the procedure or work document is not adequate. Look for these deviations. Document their existence. Make changes to the flow diagram to show their influence.

Use of Performance Indicators

The following list presents a few performance indicators in current use. For each indicator, the purpose and definition is provided, along with a discussion of pros and cons of each. The intent is not to validate or dismiss any of these, only to provide cautions in their use. Readers are invited to follow our analysis and determine how some of these might be used or adapted for their particular situation. The analysis should also serve to show how difficult it really is to derive a true performance indicator.

One of the real problems of performance indicators lies in their nature: They are often ratios. This is deliberately done to show a relationship. However, as stated, ratios are comprised of two numbers. The ratio can change because one or both numbers change. It may not change if both numbers change proportionally. Care is therefore required in interpreting these ratios.

It is also necessary to remember two other basic constraints. First, with counts, importance may not be considered. One major problem is the same as one minor. The numbers can also be artificial. For example, it is a simple matter to reduce the number (or increase) the count of audit findings by splitting or joining them in the write-up. The second problem lies in what the indicator is really supposed to show. How should readers interpret an increase in the number of reported nonconformances? It may be an increase in problems or it may be that the system has been sharpened.

The last caution is perhaps the most important. Most companies fail to baseline their indicators. They do not relate them to industry experience, stated goals, or any other measure. What should be the lost work days or amount of rework? The answer differs by industry and situation. The advice is to obtain a relative measure as soon as possible to gauge performance (process capability study). Otherwise, it becomes a guessing game. Let's look at some of these performance indicators. The first two deal with safety: One has potential, the other is in need of considerable rethinking.

Example 1: Lost Work Days (Lost Time Accident Rate)

Purpose: To measure the progress in improving industrial safety performance for personnel permanently assigned to the facility. This indicator measures the number of accidents serious enough to require time off from work.

Definition: Number of incidents for all facility personnel involving days away from work per 200,000 person-hours worked (100 person-years).

Comments: This is not a particularly bad indicator of safety performance, with the following cautions. This indicator is severely limited to one facility or operation (or a group of very similar activities). As you combine several operations with very different hazard levels, the indicator can quickly lose any meaning. It also suffers from other ratio problems described previously. For example, is one worker who was severely injured and away from the job 100 days the same as 100 workers who each lost one day each? Note that this particular indicator has a reverse logic: the lower the ratio, presumably the better the performance. The authors always prefer forward-looking or positive indicators. In this case, it would be the number of (available) person-days worked. Incidentally, there is enough information on this indicator to define a baseline and show relative performance levels. These should be included in any presentation or discussion.

Example 2: Safety Violations

Purpose: To monitor the adequacy of facility training programs which emphasize compliance with industrial safety standards, procedures, and practices intended to ensure conduct of activities in a safe workplace. This indicator is intended to be a measure of the effectiveness of the safety culture and discipline of the management and staff of the facility.

Definition: The total number of items of noncompliance with Occupational Safety and Health Administration (OSHA) Standards.

Comments: This indicator has serious problems. First, the logical connection between OSHA violations and training seems specious. Most OSHA findings have to do with facility conditions, others are based on operating procedures. Second, this indicator is based on the number of findings, which depends on how they are framed (discussed earlier). Third, the number of findings will be based on the number of inspector visits, which is also not considered. Also, the scope and nature of these inspections can vary. There is no baseline provided. This indicator would need serious rework before it could be considered useful in measuring performance.

We will now look at some operational performance indicators. Once again, their usefulness will be examined.

Example 3: Unplanned Safety Function Actuations

Purpose: To monitor progress in reducing the number of instances of significant abnormal facility conditions, requiring the actuation of facility safety functions (equipment/systems). In addition, this indicator monitors the unnecessary exercising of facility safety functions, due to spurious or inadvertent signals, which could result in those functions not being available when needed. Limiting the number of unplanned safety function actuations indicates that an adequate margin of safety is being maintained.

Definition: The number of unplanned actuations of any safety function or facility safety systems that occur when an actuation set point for a safety function is reached or when a spurious or inadvertent signal is generated and major equipment is actuated or demanded. *Unplanned* means that the actuation was not part of a planned test or evolution.

Comments: This indicator has some potential, but requires additional information. Readers should recognize its dependency upon design conditions as well as operation of the facility. It has no baseline, which gives no indication of how long the facility is in operation (or not). It also does not distinguish between major and minor shutdowns. This measure, without further definition and depending upon its use, can lead to personnel bypassing safety systems. This is counter to its intent.

Example 4: Violations of Operating Procedures

Purpose: To monitor the adequacy of facility training programs which emphasize compliance with procedures that are intended to ensure safe and effective facility operations. This indicator is intended to be a measure of the effectiveness of the safety culture and discipline of the management and staff of the facility.

Definition: The number of instances where a failure of personnel to follow operating procedures resulted in a reportable occurrence.

Comments: This is not even a real performance indicator. It is a compliance indicator. The assumption is that following procedures will result in proper operation. This may be true in some cases. It has no baseline. In addition, it is not clear how violations of procedures will be reported. Serious problems here might reflect on the safety culture or discipline or it might be an indicator that the system (and procedures) are flawed. This indicator needs to go back to the drawing board.

Finally, a couple of systematic indicators.

Example 5: Open Audit Issues

Purpose: To measure the responsiveness of facility management and staff to findings, concerns, and recommendations from oversight and line program assessments. This performance indicator provides an indication of the management control and staff attitude toward improvements in the conduct of facility activities and openness to suggestions of outside organizations.

Definition: The total number of findings, including concerns and recommendations requiring corrective actions, by oversight assessments and line program self -assessments for which contractor corrective actions have not been completed at the time of the report.

Comments: This indicator is a real loser. It suffers from all the problems previously mentioned. The authors have seen backlogs of literally hundreds of trite, meaningless issues pile up, the majority of which, if not all, are not even worth fixing. Perhaps if combined with an importance or risk value, this indicator might have some value. Like the previous indicator, it tends to be more of a compliance than effectiveness or performance indicator.

Example 6: Corrective Maintenance Backlog

Purpose: To measure the effectiveness of the programs in place to ensure necessary and timely repairs are made to facility equipment. Maintaining a small backlog is an indication of management control and staff concern regarding the material and safety status of the facility. It is a measure of effective planning, scheduling, coordination, and materials management. Keeping long-standing deficiencies to a minimum enhances the ability to operate the facility and encourages facility personnel to report deficiencies.

Definition: The percentage of open corrective maintenance work requests, including those requiring facility or process shutdown, that are greater than three months old at the end of the reporting period. Corrective maintenance may include minor modifications if performed under a corrective maintenance work request.

Comments: Readers will recognize that this indicator has several underlying, but powerful components that are not listed. One is facility design and the other is age. It also depends on how a corrective action request is defined. There are major overhauls and there are lightbulb replacements. There are repairs to bathroom faucets and to major safety systems. This indicator, like most of the others, needs further work to be useful.

The purpose in providing these indicators and then commenting on them is to demonstrate clearly just how difficult it is to derive a meaningful performance indicator. When devising an indicator, look at it in the daylight. Turn it over and around to examine it carefully. Ask yourself: What does it really represent? How does it work? Is it a measure of performance? To answer this, improved (actual) performance should make the indicator move in the desired direction. Does it show what you want or need to know? Last, remember that any indicator must have a goal or baseline to truly gauge its relative performance level.

Defining Performance Goals

We are using the word *goals* here a little differently than when we discussed planning. It might be aptly termed *milestones*. During the fieldwork, it is often necessary to break down performance into measurable pieces. A project, for example, might have several stages. The problem arises in defining these stages in terms of performance, rather than the usual criteria. Too often, programs or projects are defined in terms of dollars, person-hours, or schedule with no performance milestones identified. Progress is reported in terms of person-hours or dollars expended versus budget. The assessor cannot gauge the performance goals against this kind of measure.

Better measures, although not without their own problems, are tied to process or activity milestones. An example of this follows for product design (for simplicity, we have assumed satisfactory completion of each step).

- Marketing efforts complete
- Design criteria to engineering
- Engineering review of criteria complete
- Preliminary design complete
- Cost estimates complete
- Final preliminary product review
- Final design complete
- Manufacturability review complete

- First-piece assembly

- Manufacturing specifications complete

This list could be expanded to define subactivity milestones within each category. It can also be constructed for any other type of process or activity. Even previously fuzzy things like writing computer programs can be handled in this fashion. It is called *function point analysis*. Instead of using the previously mentioned criteria of person-hours or dollars expended or lines of computer code written, a number of program functional points are predefined. Much like our product design example, it provides performance milestones. These provide tangible points for measurement of actual performance. What were some of the problems alluded to earlier? One is defining successful completion of these activities. For example, the preliminary design could be finished, but inadequate. This is where the performance assessment really kicks in.

Another technique is *case-based reasoning*. It uses accumulated experience to build selection logic. For simple applications, the activities can be listed with three color codes assigned: green, yellow, and red. The colors correspond to those on a traffic light. Green indicates clear sailing or an okay to proceed, yellow advises caution, and red tells you to stop or watch out. The pattern is analyzed, with particular attention given to those activities coded yellow or red. These are the potential and historical problem areas. New activities are added or deleted as the process knowledge increases. The color coding assigned each subactivity may also change. Previous problems with a similar activity may be assumed for a new activity. It is a highly visual means of alerting assessors to those areas requiring closer scrutiny.

Being in Focus

In effectiveness and performance-based assessments, the actual fieldwork is as important as the planning. Assessors must carefully observe all that is going on. They should identify all undocumented activities and self-correcting mechanisms. When significant issues arise, the team must decide how best to proceed given this new information. The fieldwork must be sufficient to allow later root cause analysis to determine the real obstacles to improvement. For those familiar with the more formal compliance audits, the assessment will seem more fluid and less structured. This is to be expected. Effectiveness or performance measurement and evaluation are harder to do. To analyze activities properly, technical competence and familiarity with the activity or process is needed. Good fieldwork makes the later analysis and framing of results easy. It is sometimes difficult to predict accurately how long this phase of the assessment will take. When estimating, it may be wise to err on the safe side. Allow a little longer to follow your nose wherever it goes.

7

Presenting the Results

What's gone and what's past help should be past grief.
—William Shakespeare, *The Winter's Tale,* Act III, Scene ii,
Line 223

Classifying and Prioritizing

When the fieldwork is completed, the next phases of the assessment consist of analyzing the results and preparing the preliminary and final report. One of the biggest chores will be sorting out all the information the team has gathered. Some filtering and condensing may have occurred during the field activities. This will make the task easier. Figure 7.1 shows one way to do this. It lists issues covered during the assessment by the assigned, contributory causes. Patterns which emerge may be used to focus additional analysis.

Compliance, effectiveness, and performance items should be separated. In Figure 7.1, this can be done by using *C, E,* or *P* as the entries in the cells rather than *X*'s or checks. Different issues could also be color coded differently. The method used is less important than the reason for doing so. The findings and results need to be prioritized. They will later be presented in this fashion. The purpose is to separate the wheat from the chaff.

Issue	ASSIGNED ROOT CAUSE(S)																	Predominant Root Cause
	Work practice	Training/qualifications	Organization/planning	Communications	Supervision	Management methods	Resource allocation	Change management	Physical conditions	Man/machine/interface	Design	Procurement	Manufacture/installation	Operation	Maintenance/testing	Documentation	External	

Figure 7.1
Assessment issues and their contributory causes.

To prevent less-than-credible conclusions, the assessed organization should be involved to the extent practical. This is substantially different from the traditional compliance audit. However, this makes sense in avoiding serious objections and differences once the final assessment report is issued. Involving the assessed organization also ensures valid conclusions are drawn by the process of corroboration and validation.

In effectiveness and performance-based assessments, the purpose should be improvement. If the tone throughout the efforts has been both positive and collaborative, there is no reason to expect trouble at this stage. To the extent possible, the results are quantitative. Effectiveness and performance characteristics that were examined have been translated into measurable criteria. Qualitative issues have been minimal. All that should remain is to devise potential solutions for the issues that have been identified.

Sideways Looks

We have already suggested that, in effectiveness and performance-based assessments, developing the issue to determine its scope and nature is more important than finding more examples of the situation. The latter is more a characteristic of compliance audits. Sideways looks are needed to frame most performance issues. You must search for the process or sequence point at which the departure occurs. Alternately, the extent of needed or possible improvement must be realistically bounded.

An example might be helpful. Let's assume you have set out to improve aspects of customer returns. You note unusual (and unacceptable) behavior patterns on the part of some of the clerks. During the fieldwork, you must determine whether this is individual or collective demeanor. Further, the contributory causes and circumstances surrounding these cases need to be examined. If the cause is systemic, then other departments should be looked at for the same symptoms. Fixing or improving the situation at the local level will not be adequate. Certain issues or problems are like weeds. If you do not root them out or find all of them, they'll be back.

There is no universal rule that helps. Every issue or improvement opportunity identified must be sufficiently developed to be able to identify its true nature and extent. Sideways looks at surfaced issues will post the limits and aid in pattern recognition. They will isolate and define the issue and are vital in developing an appropriate solution.

Developing Solutions

Objectivity and attention to detail are essential to determine the nature, extent, and circumstances of an issue. The team must collect all available pertinent information and evidence during direct observations in the field. Root cause analysis techniques are used to minimize bias and other subjective errors. The next step is to devise potential solutions. Solutions can be viewed as being required by problems. Rather than this negative outlook, we will also define a solution as identifying the best opportunity for improvement. If we were weather forecasters, we would forecast "partly sunny" rather than "mostly cloudy."

Developing solutions to issues is extremely flexible. There are few rules and constraints. Subjectivity during this phase should be expected, but minimized. Recognizing and then counteracting this limitation has the same effect as pure sunlight reportedly has on a vampire. Old, unyielding, and sometimes counterproductive responses crumble into dust. First, we will look at personal differences in developing solutions. Everyone has a favorite remedy for a cold. Surprisingly, they all seem to work. Having sorted this out, we will then provide some advice on the process of developing solutions.

Personal Differences in Problem Solving

Developing solution(s) to issues or problems involves focused thinking. It converges on the issue and its probable cause. It results in ways to do it better. According to psychologists, quality of thinking is related to an individual's ability to

- Represent various aspects of the situation by symbols or concepts
- Develop new relationships and meanings
- Manipulate and organize these meanings
- Synthesize the results in rational conclusions

Thinking ranges between two extremes. The first is reasoning, which is highly directed and focused. The second is autism, which is largely self-directed and imaginative. Covering the entire range between these two extremes will provide a variety of potential solutions, from the most obvious to the most creative. Most people think in a usual, predictable fashion. This depends on their background, experience, and personality. They tend to come up with solutions or answers unique to their point of reference. There's nothing wrong with this. It's who we are. When you're a hammer, every problem looks like a nail. Recognizing these individual preferences is the first step. The next step is to override this potential limitation. To maintain balance and secure the widest range of possible solutions, the entire team needs to be involved. Brainstorming, nominal group techniques, and other means should be employed. Readers interested in these and other group dynamics processes will find a number of books on these subjects. Collective thinking (*groupthink* in 1960s terms) will result in a predictably better outcome. The intent is not to limit individual contribution, but to encourage all individuals to provide input.

The Process
Basic steps for developing solutions follow the classical scientific method

1. Become familiar with all the aspects of the issue or problem and its cause.
2. Derive a number of tentative solutions.
3. Assemble as much detail as is needed to clearly define what it will take to implement these solutions.

4. Evaluate the suggested solutions.

5. Objectively test and revise the solutions.

6. Develop a final list of potential solutions.

Some Pitfalls

The following common pitfalls should be avoided. This list is far from complete. Hopefully, by recognizing some of these traps, teams can avoid them. Remedies are suggested.

Binary Thinking: This trap is the failure to recognize degrees of value in any solution. The term *binary* implies two states. Binary thinking infers any answer or solution must be either right or wrong. Black or white; there are no shades of grey.

Remedies: Most solutions have some value. Some just have more than others. All roads lead to Rome. Some are a little longer or more torturous. A few may even be practically impassable. Remember a diamond in the rough. With some minor modification, an idea destined for the junk pile may end up as a prize jewel.

Incomplete or Faulty Information: This pitfall occurs when all the facts are not considered. The information may be incomplete or inadequate. This pitfall may also occur when faults are not detected. This pitfall is particularly easy to fall into when the information seems to fit. This is called a *Type II error* in decision making: accepting something to be true when, in fact, it is not.

Remedies: Take nothing for granted. Until you are satisfied, assume there is something missing, something you should know, but haven't yet been told. Be suspicious. Examine the facts. Sort out those you are absolutely sure of. Put the rest on this same pile only when you're convinced you have all the information. Use the same caution that you would use when buying a used car from someone you don't know.

Desire to Believe: This predisposition toward certain facts or conclusions is based solely on psychological values or beliefs. The verdict precedes the trial. It is already in, regardless of any evidence to the contrary. This category of pitfall includes foregone conclusions, self-fulfilling prophecies, generalizations, stereotypes, and rigid preconceptions.

Remedies: Become a fact agnostic. Accept nothing that can't be proven or observed. Constantly check your thinking for any predeterminations. If the only worthwhile solution was "what you always knew it should have been," you may have already fallen into this trap. Check your baggage at the counter.

Failure to Develop Alternate Hypotheses: This is like putting all the eggs in one basket. All the facts can be explained by one reason or cause. One solution will fit all circumstances. One size fits all. There is little or no attempt to consider other explanations or possibilities. This trap can be sprung by a desire to believe. It can also happen because other solutions are not encouraged.

Remedies: Disengage your mind clutch. Mentally freewheel for a while. Look sideways. See if anything appears in the rearview mirror. Walk away from the problem for a while. Stare at the ceiling. Get a cup of coffee or whatever. Then come back with fresh perspective.

Making the Pieces Fit the Puzzle: Who has not done this? The human eye (actually it's the brain) fills in missing information to create a familiar pattern. Illusionists rely on this. False impressions appear plausible. Nonetheless, people cannot float in air; we are denser. This trap is deadliest when some predetermined (or preferred) solution influences its development.

Remedies: Check logic paths. Does it really proceed smoothly from point A to point B, and all the way to point N? Is there anything that is obviously missing? Check for all the facts.

Correlation Versus Causation: The observation that two (or more) things seem to be related to each other does not guarantee they are. Relatives sometimes come to accept this explanation when faced with explaining an embarrassing family member. Things may turn out to be influenced by yet another, perhaps unknown, factor.

Remedies: The observation that a train leaves the station every time the clock strikes eight o'clock does not mean that the clock striking causes the train to leave. This whole cause-and-effect thing is a big problem for philosophers, too. So don't feel too bad. Try the relationship in the following type of sentence: It is obvious, even to the most casual observer, that arms must cause legs since the number of arms and the number of legs are so highly correlated. If it doesn't sound even remotely logical, try again.

While the rules of formal logic are technical, the proposed solution(s) can also be evaluated using a simple test. Does the stated conclusion reasonably follow from the stated premises? Does the proposed solution reasonably line up with the original issue or problem and its cause? (See Figure 7.2.)

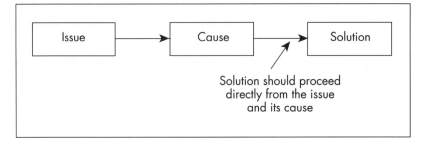

Figure 7.2
Lining up the solution.

Another way to visualize the relation of issues and solutions is a matrix. Issues, contributory or root causes, and proposed solutions are listed in Figure 7.3. The matrix is useful in identifying specific fixes that are repetitive and can be combined. Other columns may be added if desired. For example, you can add columns for evaluation, such as cost, probability of occurrence, or success.

Issue	Root Cause	Solution

Figure 7.3
Solutions matrix.

Devising Solutions

The previous section pointed out some of the traps to avoid when devising potential solutions. The following section talks about crafting solutions.

The first step should be to recheck the definition of the issue or problem and the assigned cause. Reexamine the evidence from the fieldwork. Often an issue has evolved from its original description. Review the planned goal. Make sure you clearly understand exactly what it represents. What started out as an improved deposit slip may have turned into a paperless transaction. Shortcuts taken here will limit the choice of an effective solution and thereby seriously affect the overall effort.

Once this review is completed, the next step is to formulate possible solutions. This should include not only those that are obvious, but also those that are novel and imaginative. Brainstorming is an effective technique to identify possible solutions. How many possible solutions are appropriate? Edison unsuccessfully tried more than 1200 different materials for an electric lightbulb filament. Chided for failing that many times, Edison simply replied, "I have discovered 1200 materials that don't work." He then proceeded to find one that did. The number of proposed solutions will be influenced by the nature of the particular issue, its cause, and its importance. The more ideas, generally the better. The primary rule of brainstorming is not to constrain the flow of ideas. Make no attempt to evaluate or otherwise sort the ideas during the process. The next idea might very well turn out to be the best.

Recall the true story of the trailer truck wedged under a bridge. The driver had either ignored or missed the usual sign advising the height of the upcoming underpass. The momentum of the vehicle caused the semitrailer to become firmly stuck. Traffic was backed up for miles. The driver, police, state engineers, and onlookers all offered possible solutions. Some were plainly destructive (such as cutting apart the trailer). None appeared particularly attractive. Then a little boy, who had been watching intently, asked: "Why don't you let some air out of the tires?" They had overlooked the simplest idea of all.

Another source of potential solutions is benchmarking. Find out what others have done in similar situations. Borrow or stretch ideas. Sometimes elegant solutions come from areas or disciplines outside our immediate area of expertise. A dynamite way of posting accounts might be easily adapted to keeping track of engineering changes. At other times, you can look at sister activities. Look at the newer, more novel concepts in public education adapted from private sector training. Many of these have been borrowed by trainers from the military (public sector).

Develop a wider view. Avoid predetermined or unnecessary restrictions. When it is remotely possible that a particular solution might work, include it. Any art teacher will tell you that sometimes a different perspective will make an otherwise dull picture interesting.

Consider solutions to be either long versus short term and targeted versus generic. For example, personnel training is often suggested as a potential solution. The downside is that most training tends to wear off. Problems with retention, personnel turnover, and replacement impact its value as a long-term solution. If training is to be a long-term solution, the training program design needs to include refresher sessions and updates as required, after any initial training. The short- and long-term aspects of any proposed solution must be addressed to be complete.

Solutions should also be examined in terms of their specificity. Is it targeted to the specific issue or does it represent a broader, more generic solution? Let's use our training example again. You might provide toolbox or on-the-job training for craftspeople on the proper way to lock out and tag equipment when removing it from operation for maintenance or repair. This training is targeted at a fairly specific issue. A more generic approach might include this specific topic (along with others) in safety training. This might be better when evidence suggests a general lack of understanding regarding safety practices. However, it would be an overreaction to conduct a more elaborate training program than the situation suggests is necessary.

Look at any proposed solution in terms of the importance of the issue and the particular situation. Consider both time frame and specificity for proper context. Also recognize that what works well in one situation may be entirely inadequate in another. As one commercial states: There are no easy answers, just intelligent choices.

Some Aids

The following advice may aid in developing a better list of potential solutions.

Reduce Each Solution to Its Most Basic Form: Quite often the way a solution is stated limits other possibilities. It represents one viewpoint within a larger set. For example, *putting on socks and shoes* is contained in the broader statement *cover and protect your feet.* There are many other ways to cover or protect your feet than just socks and shoes. Restate the solution in a more basic or generic form. This may suggest other ideas. Look at form, fit, and function.

Write Down All Obvious Solutions First: Before going off in all directions, write these down. Otherwise you may forget to double back and check obvious solutions. This can result in overlooking perfectly good solutions. By looking this list over, it may help you think of others.

Write Down Any Other Ideas That Come Up: Before getting into the detail of any of these solutions, write down any other ideas that occur to you. Do a little freewheeling.

Replace Factors and See if a New Solution Emerges: Remove one or more factors that must be considered. This sometimes helps you see whole new possibilities. Suppose Edison had intended to develop a better candle.

Use Branching to Find More Alternatives: Draw a simple diagram like the one in Figure 7.4. It will help develop alternatives. Continue branching as long as you can. New possibilities may emerge. Let's consider the simple situation of discovering a flat tire on your automobile. The most obvious answer is to replace it with the spare. However, drawing a diagram shows there are many alternatives. Depending upon the situation, one may be better than another.

Consider Any Constraints: Looking at constraints helps focus and may suggest additional solutions. Consider the previous example of putting on socks and shoes. Let's assume the solution statement has been reduced to its more basic form: cover the feet. Then we add the factor of travel in deep snow. The constraint implies that street shoes, sneakers, sandals, or the like need revision. Snowshoes or some method to distribute the person's weight need to be added.

Once a set of solutions has been derived, the next step will be to make sure they are adequately described so as to allow others to understand and evaluate them.

Preparing Solutions

Once the list of potential solutions has been developed, the remaining tasks are framing them and adding information/criteria for their evaluation. The final version of a proposed solution should include

- A clear statement with the essential features identified
- Its attributes and characteristics
- Qualitative or quantitative measures for evaluation

Framing the Issue
Fieldwork during an effectiveness or performance-based assessment will result in a number of observations by the team.

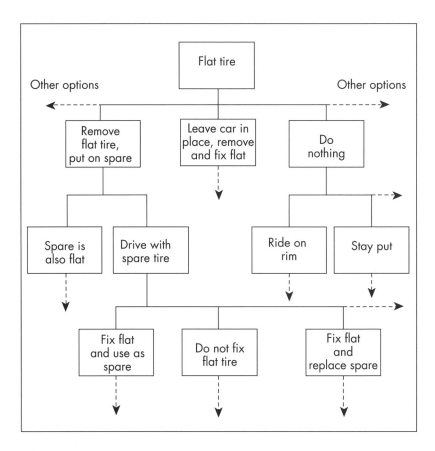

Figure 7.4
Alternate solutions diagram—flat tire.

These should be described as meticulously as possible. All pertinent data and information must be carefully collected and recorded. These will usually have the form suggested by the plan, assessment strategy, and lines and method of inquiry.

At some point, surfaced issue(s) need to be framed. It is important that the issue be stated in terms of its effect on operation or performance. The intended audience is those responsible for the activity or process. The issue must be stated in these terms. For example, noncompliance to procedures is not necessarily an effectiveness or performance issue, of and by itself. In terms of effectiveness or performance, it is an indeterminate statement. The question "What does this mean?" should be anticipated. In fact, not following inadequate procedures may be a plus. The relationship must be made between not following procedures and the activity or process. Otherwise the (legitimate) response could be "So what?"

State the issue in real life, operational terms. Not following procedures results in

- People not knowing what to do
- Extreme variation in the results obtained
- Missing important subactivities
- Doing things wrong
- Taking considerably longer to perform the task
- Slipped deadlines

These are the nub, the core of the issue. These are real problems that can result from not following procedures. They have been quantified in operation-speak. This is where the rubber meets the road. It is these effects that are the real concern.

These effects cannot be inferred or suggested. Not following procedures does not guarantee any of the previous problems. The observations must support and validate these. If previous fieldwork was not sufficient to state confidently that (for example) deadlines have slipped, then further proof or evidence is needed. No suppositions are allowed. Nothing will destroy credibility faster than this.

On the positive side, thinking observations through in this fashion can provide focus and crystallize otherwise fuzzy issues. The advice is that unless you can frame the issue in the manner that will really get attention, it may not be all that important. In that case, put it in the "oh, by the way" pile or forget it entirely.

Determining the Essential Features

It is important to capture the essence of the proposed solution. Solutions need to relate directly to the planned goals. The solution should be described in summary form, with any essential features. If several options are included within a particular proposed solution, they should be clearly indicated. This is essential for presentation to management. Stating the proposed solution in this fashion may also disclose omissions or needed redirection. This is the final polish. It may reveal defects that a little added refinement (repolishing) can easily remove.

Providing the Attributes

Attribute, as used herein, is vaguely similar to the term used in quality control, but far broader. Attributes are characteristics or properties that can be observed or measured. Attributes aid in making a choice between alternatives. This consists of linking goals and essential features to objective measures. Certain attributes may be stated on extraorganizational or accrual terms. As an example, consider the technical training provided by the armed forces. This training is necessary based on the increased complexity of weapons systems (direct need), but has also produced a supply of technically competent individuals in the subsequent civilian job market (subsequent benefit). The magnitude of the required training effort by the armed forces is obviously influenced by high (and vocational) school curricula. This is recognized and demonstrated by the armed forces' admonition to stay in school prior to entry into the service. On the other hand, the training provided has, in many cases, lessened the required training by private industry. These are (properly) included as relevant attributes in recruitment efforts.

Developing Quantitative and Qualitative Measures

A quantitative measure can be represented by a scale, measurement, or range of values. This measure should be highly correlated to the attribute, much as test results should indicate the level of knowledge of a subject. For example, test validity remains a continuing concern to most educators. With performance, this can be even more difficult. This is the basis for skills demonstration.

In certain situations, it is sometimes difficult to assign quantitative measures to proposed solutions. Certain solutions may only be described in qualitative terms. Many social programs are an excellent example. What criteria should be applied to measure the social effects of child care support?

Certain solutions can be measured only in terms of risk avoidance or mitigation. This is especially true for events that have not yet happened. Their occurrence can only be probabilistically estimated.

Trying Out the Solutions

Review potential solutions with the affected organizations. The organization(s) responsible for corrective, preventive, or adaptive actions often provide valuable input. They may suggest other solutions that have not yet been considered. They will eventually have to buy into the solution for it to work. Being part of the process will develop a sense of ownership.

Affected organizations may be able to identify practical constraints to the proposed solution. Rather than a watering down process, this may make the proposed solution more viable. In the real world, a less-than-perfect solution is better than none at all or one that is not implemented because it is too elaborate. This is one more example of where the art is as important as the science.

Recognizing Constraints

Will the proposed solution correct the issue or provide the intended improvement? In some instances, the proposed solution may not only be ineffective, but might worsen the situation. The authors are reminded of some of the patent cough medicines of their childhood years that not only did not lessen the coughing, but introduced nausea as a further misery. Proposed solutions must be evaluated for conditions that may restrict or constrain their effectiveness or ability to be implemented. These constraints can be embedded within the solution itself or be imposed by the present system. Consider again the previous example of personnel training as a proposed solution. Constraints that might be considered as part of the evaluation of this solution might include the following

- Will the needed training be adequately defined and effectively implemented?
- Are the needed instructors available?
- Will schedules be established and the personnel needing training be made available?

■ Will measures be provided to assess training performances?

Each proposed solution should be evaluated for possible constraints. Is the solution doable? Many proposals are unrealistic. The concept is fine, but they cannot be successfully implemented. Involving the assessed organization should eliminate most of these obstacles.

The Value of Perfect Information

Decision theory provides an interesting concept: that of having perfect information. Perfect information means that all the facts and all the potential difficulties or consequences of a decision are known prior to the decision being made. There is no uncertainty involved. In real life, there is always some uncertainty involved in every decision. The cost of obtaining better (even if not perfect) information can be higher than the consequences of a wrong choice. The time required to obtain this added information might be unreasonable. This could hinder decisions from being made in a timely fashion. Perfect information should not be a prerequisite to developing proposed solutions. However, the team should generally attempt to get as close to this goal as practical. Learn to recognize the potential uncertainty in the assessment data and information. Attempt to provide some form of countermeasure to offset potential uncertainties where possible.

Also, recognize that personal and organizational bias may enter in, whether consciously or not. This will result in certain proposed solutions receiving higher scores. For example, when a company introduces a new product, production personnel might have a completely different perspective than marketing and sales personnel. One sees the product in terms of new opportunities or needed additions, the other simply as a new set of problems. Recognize this bias may exist. Compensate for it.

Evaluating Improvement Opportunities

This is a touchy subject. One could argue that any costs associated with improvement need not be considered, since they are absolutely vital to continued operation. Others, influenced by corporate inertia, would argue them as altogether inappropriate. Things seem just fine. The truth lies somewhere in the middle. It also depends on the current organizational health. For those already in serious trouble, the obvious benefit is just staying alive. No argument needed. For most organizations, an evaluation or measure of benefits is needed.

The simplest measures are those based upon specific, well-defined, and/or easily quantified factors, such as cost or compliance with predetermined requirements. For compliance with mandated standards, there is a built-in acceptability threshold. All proposed solutions that do not ensure compliance are automatically declared invalid.

When there are several ways to perform the same activity which provide the same results, cost (alone) may be used to differentiate these. Cost criteria are relatively straightforward. However, cost alone can often lead to false conclusions. The value of the solution should be considered. Value may or may not be directly related to cost. Cost-benefit analyses may be needed. When these benefits can be expressed in dollars, the return on investment can be calculated. For example, if training will result in increased production or result in fewer downtime hours, the costs can be compared using the same common denominator: dollars. The same is true for decreased absenteeism, increased employee retention, and so on.

However, there are also real, substantial benefits that cannot be easily expressed in dollars. Examples include corporate goodwill or social responsibility. The comparison and grading of these benefits is made on a different basis, using an aesthetic scale or other measurement scale, such as intrinsic value.

In other situations, improvements cannot be measured against any expected benefit. Examples include improvements designed to mitigate or eliminate a potential risk. Safety improvements can fall into this category. This becomes a risk-benefit evaluation. The avoidance rating becomes the significant consideration. The lower the potential for exposure to risk, the higher the rating. It is almost impossible to reduce risk to zero. The cost would be prohibitive. We live with a certain amount of risk which we consider acceptable given the situation. Consider airport security. The threat of firearms or explosives being brought onboard airline flights could be substantially reduced by full body searches, emptying all luggage, searching through all packages loaded as baggage, and so on. To do this, passengers would have to arrive for their flight several hours in advance. Although the risk would be substantially reduced, the cost of such an effort would not be worth its benefit. However, when terrorism is a real possibility, effective risk management suggests any or all of these measures are not only appropriate, but necessary and prudent.

Improvements may also be evaluated in terms of time frame. That is, how soon the benefits or their expected results will be realized. Solutions that provide the quickest results will usually be given the highest score, given the same cost and chance of success. Time frame can mean the time required to implement, the time to expect results, the lasting power, or a combination thereof.

Improvements may also be evaluated using their probability of success. Each proposed solution is assigned a chance of success or failure. Probabilities may be assigned from previous experience or similar situations. Those with a low probability of success can usually be disregarded. Even if the assigned probability of success or failure is somewhat subjective, the picture will be clearer than when each proposed solution is given an equal chance for success (which is usually assumed to be the case when no probabilities are assigned). An equal chance of success for all alternatives is not realistic, unless you are flipping a coin.

Assigned probabilities can be multiplied by quantitative units to obtain expected values. A lottery ticket could represent millions of dollars. However, the chance of winning must also be considered. When you multiply the odds of actually winning by the jackpot amount, you get the expected value. If you pay $1 for a lottery ticket with a $1 million jackpot and one in a million chance of winning, the expected value of your ticket is exactly what you paid for it.

Organizations (and individuals) face these problems all the time. Should I go to night school and get that degree? The costs in time and money and the perceived benefits are clear. No two persons will have the exact same criteria for evaluating this improvement opportunity. Decisions will be made based on importance and the particular situation. However, if you list all the circumstances and personal preferences, chances are you'll be able to predict the outcome more often than not. In a larger sense, all improvement opportunities are evaluated in this manner.

8

Developing an Action Plan
for Improvement

All lovers swear more performance than they are able, and yet reserve
an ability that they never perform; vowing more than the perfection of
ten, and discharging less than the tenth part of one.
—William Shakespeare, *Troilus and Cressida,* Act III, Scene ii,
Line 89

Most taxpayers have heard of the National Performance Review. Initiated in March 1993, the results were published in September 1993. The report is entitled *From Red Tape to Results: Creating a Government That Works Betterand Costs Less.*[1] It is of particular interest because it represents just what this book is all about. The report states that successful organizations had several things in common. They

- Cut red tape—shifting from a system based on following rules to one of achieving results

- Put the customers first—listening to them, restructuring to meet their needs, and using customer choice and competition to create incentives

- Empower employees to get results- decentralizing authority and empowering those on the front lines to make more of their own decisions and solve more of their own problems

- Cut back to basics—abandoning the obsolete, eliminating duplication, and ending special interest privileges

It is fascinating to read this report. If implemented, substantial improvements in government activities can be realized. Only time will tell whether it should have been listed as fiction. If so, the administration will not be alone. Many private sector firms have done the very same thing. Follow-through on laudable goals has faltered. Organizations have sailed into uncharted waters with few navigational aids. Quality improvement efforts are under scrutiny because the apparent burden has not produced tangible results. There is many a slip twixt the cup and the lip. The authors reiterate the reason is obvious, in fact, suggested earlier. These organizations had not prepared for the journey. Further, along the way, they disregarded navigational aids.

However, returning to the report, it is somewhat mistitled. Most of the items discussed deal with improving effectiveness rather than performance. An example of each follows, taken from the section on streamlining procurement.

One action item states: "Allow agencies to make purchases under $100,000 through simplified purchase procedures." The report explains that current law allows use of simplified procurement practices only on purchases of $25,000 or less. This initiative clearly aims at improving the effectiveness of the procurement system.

Another action item states: "Rely more on the commercial marketplace." The report adds the government can save money by buying more commercial products instead of requiring products be built to government-unique specifications. This would seem to spell the demise of $600 toilet seats. This is more a performance issue, since it revolves around equivalent form, fit, and function. Those of us who have worked in this environment recognize the value added in military specification items. Could this same concept lead to wider use by physicians of clinically equivalent (but far less costly) generic drugs? This may be one genie that's better left in the bottle (no pun intended).

However, the report is an excellent example of what we are going to cover next: a definitive, well-conceived action plan for improvement. We will assume Al Gore's team went through many of the same steps described here in preparing the plan.

Criteria for Evaluating Alternatives

Alternative improvements have only one ultimate criterion. Will they produce the desired result? To determine this, several factors will require rating. These include

- Intrinsic merit
- Planning efforts
- Implementation aspects
- Organizational climate
- Follow-through

Intrinsic Merit

This is almost self-explanatory. Does the proposed change represent a real improvement? Is it change for change's sake? Quite often, a new way of doing things may not really be much better than the old. If it's not, don't bother. The idea is doomed from the start. There will be little, if any, support from those who will have to buy into it. Remember the example of Coca-Cola with the new, improved formula. The company found that customers were, in fact, quite fond of the old, familiar taste. Facing declining sales, the company hurriedly reintroduced the previous drink, now called Classic Coke. It really happens. Make sure the idea has intrinsic merit. It makes sense and is needed.

Planning Efforts

Efforts spent in planning can reap enormous rewards. Even terrific ideas can be half-baked. Take the time to look at an idea from all aspects. Consider its main features. Use these to develop the concept. Think it through carefully. Think about timing, the way it will be introduced, all the things that may impact its implementation. Read through the following section on change and overcoming problems that may arise. Spend time with those who will be affected. Get their input. Make sure the idea can be translated into action. Refine the thought to be practical.

Implementation Aspects

This is partially covered in the previous section about planning. Make sure the delivery is good. The best lines can be ruined by poor delivery. On the other hand, sometimes problems in the material can be rectified in the hands of a good practitioner. Implementation aspects include system checks. They include people checks. In short, all resources that need to be applied should be examined for suitability. For want of a horseshoe, a kingdom can be lost.

Organizational Climate

Even solid objects can disappear in the dark. If the organizational climate does not support or encourage improvement, the effort is wasted. This is sometimes not obvious until later. Tacit approval is not sufficient endorsement. Until negative corporate inertia is overcome, little progress will be made. On a less global basis, if the affected organizations or individuals are not sold on the idea, it will likewise wither.

Follow-through

Once planted, a seed must be watered and watched over. Follow-through is crucial to ensure that improvements become firmly rooted. The changed performance must become the new mode of operation. Effective follow-up is discussed in considerably more detail later in this chapter.

Developing the Action Plan

The action plan ties together the framed issue and the goal. Between these two, a plan represents a path. It articulates specific steps that need to be followed to reach the desired performance level. The plan should be checked for

- Cause-and-effect lineup
- Doability
- Evaluation criteria
- Resource loading requirements

Cause-and-Effect Relationships

The action plan should have a final check on cause-and-effect lineup. This is similar to that previously discussed in resolving the issue, except in reverse. Plan segments should be looked at both individually and collectively to ensure the proposed action will produce the desired result. Also, could one aspect of the plan contradict or cancel another? In dealing with people, this is sometimes complicated. What is intended to produce one behavior may result in another. A good example of this can be found in censorship. Well-intentioned actions by some in forbidding or limiting exposure become an invitation or challenge to others. Posting of off-limit premises by the military is construed as a listing of hot spots to visit. In a plan, we hope to cause an effect (improved performance). Therefore, the stimulus and its reception must be examined carefully. The impact of change and its introduction is discussed in further detail later.

Doability

This term is used with apologies to the Save Our Tongue Society (SOTS). It is used to give the clearest idea of this particular attribute. The improvement plan must be reviewed to ensure it is possible; that it can be effectively implemented. Many good ideas are simply not practical. To implement others, the amount of required change exceeds the elastic limits of the organization. Known corporate inertia can smother time-dependent improvement plans. They are simply not doable in terms of the current situation. When overreach occurs, there are several options. The first would be to scale back the improvement plan somewhat, bringing it into the range of possibility. Another option is to break it down into a series of smaller increments, leaving the original goal as a stretch target. Implement the series of smaller, progressively difficult improvements. What you are doing is similar to body-building exercises. Eventually the organization will develop sufficient muscle for more difficult exercises.

Evaluation Criteria

All plans should contain evaluation criteria. These are vital to providing a measure of progress or accomplishment. If the improvement plan has none, add them. Except for compliance issues, evaluation criteria should correlate with effectiveness or performance. Examples of effectiveness criteria include that the proposed improvement results in a savings of 10 percent in person-hours, a 20 percent improvement in accuracy, or whatever. For performance criteria, an example might be that certain training results in improved job or task performance. Another example of a performance criteria would be that 20 procedures are completely revised within three months. Without criteria, it is difficult to determine where you are, how far you have come, what you have accomplished, and so forth.

Resource Loading Requirements

This aspect is far too often overlooked. The improvement plan should include a reasonably accurate inventory of the resources needed to carry it out. The resource loading should identify person-hours, budget, training requirements, situational factors, and so on. It should also catalog current person-hours available, budget changes needed, and so on whenever possible. This gives the organization an accurate feeling for the true expenditure and impact of the proposed improvement. Baselines used in the plan need complete definition. Milestones should be added to more complex plans.

Developing and Presenting the Plan

Use the following checklist of seven items to make sure the improvement plan is complete before presenting it. Efforts spent here will reap benefits later on.

1. Make sure the improvement is fully developed. Do your homework first. Collect all needed data and information. Consider who needs to be involved. Anticipate any implications or consequences. Make sure your improvement strategy is fully mature. Do a trial run (also see item 5). The most elegant solution is of little value if its implementation is not carefully planned and tried out.

2. Use a systems approach to improvement. Make sure you consider the idea in its setting. Look at the organizational climate. Does the idea need a hothouse environment or is it fairly hardy? Look at all the things that will need changing. Don't assume others will do what is necessary to make the idea work. List all the things that need to be done for the idea to work first.

3. Create a vision. Develop a clear vision of the planned improvement. Find an easy way to communicate it. Keep people informed. Listen to what others have to say and respond directly to their concerns. Quantify expected results to the degree possible. Let others know what to expect.

4. Use a positive approach. Describe the improvement in positive terms. Never place blame or try to find scapegoats. Where possible, describe alternatives or steps toward the desired goals.

5. Involve affected individuals. This should have been done all along, of course. But not everyone who will be affected may have participated in the assessment effort. Involving people obtains buy-in and gives them as much control as possible over outcomes. Develop supporters not detractors.

6. Develop incentives. The biggest incentive will be management support. The next is peer pressure. Personal payoffs or incentives can be considered. Recognition of effort can be a powerful motivator. Accountability must be clearly stated. Consequences for noncompliance are the least attractive incentives.

7. Provide training. Proper planning should identify any needed or additional training. Equip people with the necessary knowledge and skills to realize the improvement. Oth-

erwise you have not given them the tools they need to do the job. It is sad how much lip service is given training and how poor the results have (predictably) been. Companies that have viewed their employees as an investment have gotten considerable return.

Handling Change

Most of the alternatives will represent change: some minor, others major. Change and its effects must be factored into the development and presentation of the improvement plan. The word *change* has several meanings: making different, altering, transforming, replacing, abandoning, switching. Change affects both systems and persons. It can either reduce or induce personal stress. This is regardless of whether or not the proposed change is positive or negative in itself. Change influences and thereby puts stress on a system, process, or person. Because of this ability to produce stress, change must be introduced positively. Problems occur mainly because, regardless of the purpose of the change, the impact is not properly assessed.

Not all change is planned. Change can also be gradual, like the slight movement of the hands of a clock. It can be sudden, like the turning on or off of a light.

Personal Effects

Systems, procedures, and all the rest can be changed. The biggest challenge will be people. People are complex creatures. They do not always move in straight lines, read in a predictable fashion, nor respond to change in the same way. When planning or implementing change, sound advice might be that also given physicians (Hippocratic oath): "First do no harm." Introduce change positively. Reinforce and reward changed performance. Do not punish those who take longer to change.

Implementing Change

Another element of change is the manner in which change will be implemented. In analyzing how change will be introduced, ask the following questions.

"Will Change Be Implemented in a Timely Fashion?" If changes are made too slowly, the dynamics of the process or environment may nullify the desired effects. Timing is also critical. Changes introduced at an inappropriate time may escalate the issue. If changes are made too quickly, other problems arise. Timing is a crucial decision that must made during the planning of improvements. Allowance must be made for system lags and other factors.

The process of introducing and implementing change is depicted in Figure 8.1. Two aspects are shown to be important: the amount of desired change and its timing. The desired change is initiated at time zero (t_0). It is anticipated that the change be fully implemented at some point in the future, shown as t_i. The normal system response time, however, might be longer. This is shown as t_a, the actual time required for the system to accommodate the change. This system response time must be factored into the planning efforts. Otherwise there will be problems. To alter this natural response time, changes in the system itself will probably be required. The magnitude of the proposed change will also directly influence the normal system response time. Most systems have self-correcting mechanisms to allow for minor changes.

What Is the Amount of Proposed Change? The magnitude of the proposed change also needs consideration. To do this, you must know the present level or baseline. This is another reason the fieldwork is so crucial. During this effort, the team should have precisely determined this point.

Will the Change Meet the Intended Objectives? Planned improvements need to be considered in their total context. Objectives need to be carefully examined to ensure they will produce the desired effect. For example, implementing a manufacturing award program that includes only production personnel might cause dissatisfaction among others who feel unfairly excluded, such as purchasing personnel. The efforts of these personnel might be every bit as important to increased production. It is not difficult to predict that such an incomplete initiative might be counterproductive and even impair production in the long run.

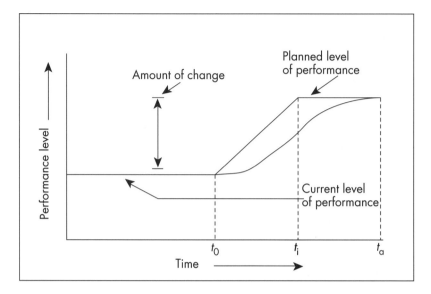

Figure 8.1
Implementing change.

Are Reinforcing Factors Considered and Included? Reinforcing factors ensure that changed levels of performance remain changed. It is very easy to slip back into the older, more familiar ways of doing business. Install validation measures to monitor how well the desired change remains in effect.

Handling Resistance to Change

Few people really like change. It is an intrusion on their comfortable, steady world. They have been accustomed to doing things in certain ways. People prefer to do things the same way each time because, after all, it took some time to learn to do it this way. Now they will have to learn all over again. Even if the proposed change makes sense, they may resist simply because it wasn't their idea. Some of the reasons for resistance are listed here.

- Lack of vision. People do not know the purpose of the change or what it consists of.

- Lack of commitment. Key individuals do not show support for the proposed change through words, actions, and personal involvement.
- Culture. The present organizational culture doesn't support change.
- Structural support. The organizational structure does not include the necessary components. For example, the company may want employee input, but first needs to install a method for employees to provide their input.
- Personal threat. People view the change as hurting their status, position, or control.
- Incentive. Payoffs (or consequences) for change don't outweigh the advantages of the status quo.
- Information. Information regarding the proposed change is incorrect, inadequate, or constantly changing. It gives the impression that the change is ill-conceived.
- Involvement and control. People affected by the change are not involved. People like to think that they have some control over their own destinies.
- Fear of the unknown. The change contains too many unknowns or risks. People hold fast to the comfort of an existing way of doing business.
- Extra work. The change will require extra work or effort. This can be fatal if the incentives for change don't outweigh the extra work involved.
- Resources. Available resources are inadequate to accomplish the proposed improvement. Extra personnel, budget, training, and so on are not considered.
- Timing. There is a lack of readiness for the change. Matters of higher priority keep putting it off.
- Political uncertainty. Some people will hold off supporting change until they determine the direction and appropriateness of responses. This is commonly referred to as the good old boy syndrome.

These reasons change (improvement) is resisted are presented so that they may be averted. Look over planned improvements and make sure these potential blocks are eliminated.

Predicting the Outcome

Proposed changes can be evaluated solely on their inherent merit. They can be worthwhile, worthless, or something in between. The planning and implementation effort can also be measured and judged in terms of its adequacy.

A simple change evaluation matrix can be constructed. The planned improvement versus its planning and implementation and their condition (adequate or less than adequate) should be shown. The resulting matrix (like the example in Figure 8.2) provides a means for predicting outcomes.

	Planning and Implementation effective	Planning and Implementation less than adequate
Good idea	Results of change good	Questionable results
Poor Idea	Questionable results	Results of change bad

Figure 8.2
Matrix of predictable outcomes.

Two of the combinations in Figure 8.2 of idea and implementation yield questionable results. When the idea is positive but the planning or implementation is negative, revising the plan, strengthening some element of implementation, or overcoming resistance to change may result in a positive outcome. In the other case, the idea was negative but implementation was positive. Take a second look at the idea. Perhaps modifying it will make the proposed change more saleable.

Prospective Change Analysis

Change analysis is one of the formal root cause analysis techniques. Briefly, change analysis analyzes events for conditions that were changed (or somehow different). It examines their effect to determine the real reason the event occurred. These same basic techniques can also be used in the forward-looking or prospective mode. Prospective change analysis predicts the effects of change. It can be used to look at the effects of change on a process, system, or organization to reveal potential situations before these changes are actually made. In the same fashion as the technique used in a reactive mode, it can look at, and define the who, what, where, when, and how of change. It consists of four basic steps.

1. Examine the present situation. Who will be affected by the change, what will change, where the change will take place, when the change will take place, and how the change will be implemented? Once again, the accuracy of the planning and fieldwork efforts are seen to be important.

2. Nature and extent of planned changes. Each of the components of the planned changes should be described in terms of people, locations, materials, processes, and proposed barriers and controls.

3. Anticipated effects. Using 1 and 2, list all known or potential effects. Participation by the assessed organization is important.

4. Evaluate the results. Analyze these potential effects and summarize the results to provide the final evaluation.

Prospective change analysis is useful for implementing and controlling change. The most expensive and regrettable problems are those that could have been avoided. Further information on the proactive use of change and barrier analysis techniques can be found in *Root Cause Analysis: A Tool for Total Quality Management.*[2]

Responding to Changes in the Plan

Most good plans are evolutionary. Nobody can look into the future and be 100 percent accurate. Start with the best strategy and recognize that it may be altered. Changes to the plan can occur for many reasons, many valid. It is critical that changes be treated in much the same way as the original plan. Incorporating these should entail the same scrutiny and analysis. We will differentiate between changes that occur during the assessment effort and those during implementation of planned improvements.

Changes During the Assessment

These are to be expected. In an effectiveness or performance assessment, the focus is on what's really happening. Despite the best preplanning and planning efforts, surprises are often in store once the fieldwork commences. Many branches occur as issues crystallize. Pursuing these as they appear is the proper approach in this type of assessment. What was known as the audit checklist is now called *potential lines of inquiry.*

Once again, the actual fieldwork for a performance-based assessment generally requires more time. This additional time is needed to allow for the more detailed observations that are required, additional activities that may need examination, and the tracing and identification of the apparent cause of any identified weaknesses. During this fieldwork, a choice will almost invariably occur as to how far to go in determining the nature and extent of a surfaced issue. Any time available will be more profitably spent on accurately framing the issue. The team may therefore engage in scope tradeoffs based on the results of the actual fieldwork. These decisions should be based on a single criterion: coverage of the more important performance issues. The fieldwork is far less structured and predictable than in compliance audits. Changes are therefore normal. In fact, it would be unusual to have none.

Changes in the Improvement Plan

Changes in the planned improvement are different. They should occur seldom, if at all, assuming the advice given previously has been followed. The planned improvement has been carefully thought through, all aspects considered and introduced properly. Required changes to installed improvements should result in lessons learned for the process; it has flaws. This does not apply to changes that evolve over time. In fact, most things need tuning up from time to time. Circumstances change and so should the plan.

Initial changes to the improvement plan should be lessened by following the steps listed previously. The most common mistake made in effectiveness or performance-based assessments is the failure to fully involve affected parties. This may be a carryover from traditional compliance-based audits. Any improvement effort should not be labeled complete until it is, in effect, fully endorsed. This fact cannot be emphasized strongly enough. We have already stated the desire for improvement must be internalized first. If this condition does not exist, the effort is wasted. The most usual tactic will then be proposed change after proposed change. This patent foot-dragging will be accompanied by a cacophony of apparently valid reasons for nonperformance. It is a losing battle. The remedy: Reexamine the entire effort. Check the goals. Make sure of the facts. Relook at the data and information. Examine the analysis and conclusions. Look at the proposed alternatives. Consider their reasonableness. Should half-measures have been used? Was the organization really ready? These and other, similar questions will help retrace the path. There may have been some unnoticed flaw(s). If these were the team's fault, fix them. If others were not involved, go back and start over. Regain what ground you have already taken. Come up with a new plan, if need be. Above all, don't give up and resort to finger pointing. That's counter to everything we're trying to accomplish.

Follow-Up

The improvement plan should contain specific evaluation criteria to be used in assessing later performance. Follow-up of action items should be monitored. In the ideal case, the improvement will become the responsibility of the affected individual or organization. Meeting milestones satisfactorily is also their responsibility. They have to make the improvement work.

However, since the performance of even one individual can affect the overall organization's efforts, others become stakeholders in a sense. While achieving goals may not be their direct concern, the failure of others to do so affects them. Some are direct customers. The rest are on the same sales team.

Traditional compliance audits had a simple remedy: Tell management or threaten to. Fear of consequences would force action. If worst came to worst, put another galley slave on that oar. Throw the old one overboard. Of course, this really never worked. It certainly doesn't today.

Recognize that problems can arise during the implementation phase. Many will be the fault of no one in particular. The idea just needs further refinement. Most ideas are like that. Remember that, in 80 percent or better of the fault situations, the blame is on the system. Assuming this to be the case gives you four to one odds that you're right. So we're starting to come up with a newer definition of follow-up than before. It now sounds more like "How's it going? Perhaps with the added "Is there anything more we can do?"

Follow-through is a nurturing process, one of ensuring that the improvement is moving forward as planned. If difficulties are encountered, the same principle applies as before. We need to remove this obstacle to improvement. If the encountered problems are serious enough, we should go back to the drawing board. Like it or not, our plan was not as perfect as we first thought. Maybe we overlooked some reasons it couldn't be implemented. Perhaps people needed training. Possibly it'll take longer than we anticipated. These are the things that effective follow-through will uncover. Of course, if the advice given at the beginning of this chapter is scrupulously followed, the follow-on look should discover only achieved goals. No problems.

Notes

1.   Al Gore. *From Red Tape to Results: Creating a Government That Works Better and Costs Less.* Report of the National Performance Review. (Washington, D.C.: Government Printing Office, 1993).

2. Paul F. Wilson, Larry D. Dell, and Gaylord F.
    Anderson, *Root Cause Analysis: A Tool for Total Quality
    Management.* (Milwaukee, Wis.: ASQC Quality Press,
    1993).

9

Implementing the Plan

*In order that people be happy in their work, these three things are
needed: They must be fit for it. They must not do too much of it. And
they must have a sense of success in it.*

—John Ruskin

The planning and conduct of effectiveness and performance-
based assessments leads to an improvement plan. Definition of
the issues that warrant attention, the development of potential
solutions, and the subsequent evaluation of these solutions
was discussed in the previous chapters. What is eventually
done with the improvement plan is equally important. Otherwise, the overall assessment and improvement planning effort
is wasted. This chapter will describe system considerations, anticipating problems, culture changes, and other aspects of implementing the improvement plan.

System Considerations

Measuring the Effectiveness of Improvements
The most often asked question is "How can I measure the effectiveness of improvement efforts?" We will explore some of
these measures, but the underlying basis for the answer is quite
simple: Did we address the identified issue or, more simply, are
we doing better?

In addition to looking at the implementation of the improvement plan (which should be straightforward), we must look at the evaluation criteria that were developed. If you recall, these were developed using effectiveness or performance measures. Be careful this is not simply a numbers game. The total number of faults or problems before and after improvement efforts would seem an easy measure. But an evaluation based solely on the frequency of problems or unwanted events is, at best, cursory. The number of reported problems can be influenced by changing the reporting system or applying different criteria. In addition, properly conducted assessments may point out problems that were not recognized as such before. Assessments make it easier to find embedded faults in the system, which should be viewed positively.

Results may have also disclosed a number of other potential performance issues. This early identification should be considered a benefit to the organization. What may be more important than the number of remaining issues may be their type. Some specific suggestions to help measure the effectiveness of installed improvements follow.

Initial and Periodic Assessments of the System(s)

Auditing guidelines suggest that any program, system, or project should be audited *at least once* during its duration or annually, whichever is less. The guidelines further point out that the initial system audit should be conducted as soon as is possible. Although we are not talking about formal audits, these same guidelines make sense when discussing assessments of installed improvements. Naturally, the effectiveness of the installed improvement should be evaluated as soon as possible after its initial implementation. Some of the obvious checklist questions are

- Have the goals and objectives been identified clearly?
- Has management buy-in and support been obtained?
- Have expectations been clearly communicated to all participants?
- By what criteria and how often will the results be evaluated?

- Was the resource loading appropriate?

- Is an appropriate response being achieved?

- Has the original issue been resolved?

This list can be expanded or modified for your particular organization, but it gives some idea of evaluation measures that can be applied. Note that the questions listed constitute an assessment based more on results than the mechanics of the system. Judging the actual improvement requires the application of standards which are based on achievement. A performance assessment looks at substance, rather than form. It is more likely to involve relative values based on external considerations, such as client satisfaction. If customer needs are still not being met, clearly something is wrong. While the system appears to be working well, it is still not properly focused or targeted.

Implementation of Required Improvements
There is a relatively straightforward means to determine the effectiveness of program or system improvements. Focus on the results. The evaluation should not be upon the elegance of the techniques utilized nor the prescription provided the process, but upon the outcomes. Have we increased client satisfaction? Are we doing better? Are we recognizing and solving problems in a timely and effective manner? Are we preventing their recurrence?

It follows then that the results of an effective performance analysis, coupled with the necessary improvements, should result in noticeable betterment of the process or activity. If the number and severity of surfaced problems or unwanted events has been drastically reduced, then the efforts may be judged successful. If even slight progress is seen in that direction, the effort could be considered potentially successful, with study made to discover hang-ups. However, if either of these two positive indications is absent, it is reasonable to assume that the efforts have not produced the intended results. What then? The answer is obvious. Go back and find out what's wrong. Take a fresh look. If necessary, change the system.

Concepts of Evolutionism Versus Creationism

There is a tendency to assume that everything must be right before any improvement is introduced. And to the extent that they can be, this is a good philosophy. However, nothing is perfect. Delaying the implementation of systems such as performance assessments, improved problem reporting systems, root cause analyses, and other similar mechanisms makes no sense at all. In doing so, the organization members are playing blind-man's bluff. They become unaware of potentially significant problems surrounding them. They miss the chance to be all they can be.

The importance of planning integrated systems cannot be overemphasized. The chances of success increase dramatically. The adequacy of any improvement can be judged only during implementation, whereas its effectiveness while on the drawing board can only be estimated. Given the current competitiveness situation, you can be blamed for not trying.

Management textbooks also recommend the installation of short-term improvements, rather than to accumulate them or wait for the one big improvement. There is probably no large, truly effective system that was created perfectly. Deficiencies noted during the initial implementation or subsequent operation phases are translated into system changes that are required and made. The process is therefore one of evolution.

Two points emerge. The first is that any improvement, when first installed, is likely to contain some embedded flaws. Accept this as plain fact and do not allow it to become the reason for delaying the plan's implementation. The second is that, as these expected flaws emerge, do not disregard them. Use them to fine-tune the system. Recognize that effective systems evolve. They were not created that way. Sometimes, changes will be needed just because time and conditions change. The installed improvement itself might force further change by identifying less-than-adequate organizational, process, or activity conditions. That's definitely okay. Remember the objective is continuous improvement.

Checking Results of Specific Improvements

Periodically revisit installed improvements. This reexamination is important for two reasons. The first critical objective is to determine the effectiveness of the improvements. Use some of the questions listed previously. Unless this check is performed, you are operating an open-loop system. No feedback is provided. The improvement may require modification. Circumstances may have changed. Another reason for checking is to determine if further improvement is needed. There is also a dark side. Sometimes well-intended improvement efforts can actually reduce the effectiveness of other processes or activities. More ominously, they may even make matters worse. There is the curious logic here that two rights could end up making a wrong.

This wider view leads to the question: Is the overall system, including any improvements, effective in meeting and exceeding customer/client expectations? Evaluating the further need for improvements is every bit as important as installing them properly in the first place.

Anticipating Problems

The easiest problem to solve is the one that does not occur. Anticipating and thereby avoiding problems is a higher level skill than solving them. While we have stressed technique, emphasized proper corporate culture, and discussed how to use corporate inertia positively, we also recognize we live in the real world. Much of this will take time and effort. There will be roadblocks put in the way. Rather than take the easy way out, planned improvements must be viewed as an imperative. It should not be a question of why, what, or where. The only concerns should be how and when.

Facing the Facts
One of the most prevalent reasons improvement plans do not work is simply that they are not utilized or applied. Properly done, considerable effort has already been expended in gathering pertinent information, analyzing the issue, devising potential solutions, and then selecting the most appropriate solution. What often is wrong is not what was done, but the answer itself. Nobody likes the solution. It is usually inopportune or unpolitical to thwart the assessment effort during the conduct and reporting phase. It is better to wait until things

have settled down and then simply drag your feet during the implementation phase.

For example, it is reasonable to expect that a fair proportion of surfaced issues will be traced to less-than-adequate management methods. While the percentage of poor management methods may differ from one organization to another, they are generally the predominant root cause of organizational problems. Since the assessment results and accompanying improvement plans are given to management, this is unwelcome news. After all, management is supposed to solve problems, not cause them.

A certain amount of bias and predisposition toward solutions is also to be expected. There may be traditional or accepted reasons for problems that have to be set aside. There may even be suggestions as to how the assessment may be improved. While there may be perspectives that, up to this point, were not introduced, changes or alterations to the improvement plan should not be allowed. The advice here is simple: Having done all you should do, face the facts even if you don't like or agree with them.

This obvious and rather straightforward advice might seem unnecessary. However, it has already been pointed out that disregarding or deviating from the improvement plan is the reason most effectiveness and performance-based assessments fail. They fail in practice, not principle.

Failure to act on needed improvements is perhaps even worse than not recognizing the need for them in the first place. First, considerable effort and time has been expended for no worthwhile purpose. If the organization is not prepared to walk the talk, then it should probably avoid doing something that will only be disregarded or alibied away. TQM is based on continuous improvement. Recognition of these identified opportunities for improvement is a necessary ingredient. If this problem is noted, then the organizational degree of readiness needs to be reexamined.

Culture Issues

We have already discussed the role of corporate culture. When implementing improvement, an organization's environment can become strained. Its true nature can be revealed. Often this can spell the demise of well-intentioned efforts to introduce needed improvements. We have coined the term *corporate inertia*. This inertia resists movement and it also tends to continue it once in motion. The challenge will be to overcome the initial resistance and then to encourage forward motion, once started.

No discussion of this subject can proceed very far without looking into rewards/punishment aspects. Most often, these are implicit or must be guessed at. Few organizations will state any new ideas are forbidden or making mistakes is okay. If anything, the reverse will be the stated policy. However, the practice may not support these concepts. Unfortunately, in most organizations, the real meaning is clear to employees. The result is that performance moves into the acceptable norm range and stays there. Keep your nose clean. Do enough to maintain your job, but little more. Take no chances. If you want to get promoted or a raise, move to the higher level, but stay within the range. Move to the front of the pack, but don't leave it.

The results have been predictable. So also have been the consequences. Perhaps the newer concepts of disembodied corporations and fluid task teams will eventually change this. Sort of like the younger, more vigorous growth that occurs when large trees fall in the forest. Most corporations will need to shed the old skin. Readers face a choice: They can sit around waiting for this to happen or become an effective change agent. If the corporate environment needs improvement, pitch in and make it happen. After all, it's a collective thing. Like some chemical reactions, all that may be needed is a catalyst.

Implementing Change Effectively

Having decided some change is needed for improvement, readers are reminded of its two basic components: the idea itself and how it is implemented. It is the latter that will be discussed here. Refining the idea to its most perfect form has already been covered. Remember the sage advice by John Ruskin at the beginning of this chapter. In order for people's (and hence, organizations') performance to improve, three things are needed.

1. Employees must be fit for work.
2. Employees must not work too hard.
3. Employees must be successful at work.

In our terms, the individuals and the organization must be ready for change. The improvement must be fully resource loaded. Any needed training must be accomplished. The amount of change must be commensurate with the goals and the ability of the organization to implement it. Finally, the individuals and organizations need a perceived benefit, if not specific rewards, as an incentive. Things apparently haven't changed all that much in 100 years.

Managing Change

Change is necessary for improvement. Required change must be managed properly. Chapter 8 discussed the need to understand, control, and predict the effects of change. Installed improvements and the organization itself may need revision as time passes or conditions change. It is generally unwise to take medicine much beyond achieving a state of well-being. It is likewise advisable to consider revisiting some of these treatments. It may be necessary to tighten or open limits, adjust the previous baseline, or otherwise fine-tune installed improvements.

However, when doing this, treat any and all revisions as a new issue and solution. Only by subjecting each revision (however seemingly small) to the same rigor as that accorded the initial issue and solution will there be sufficient assurance of its correctness.

Natural Variation

Key to defining needed improvements as well as installing them adequately is understanding the natural or normal variation inherent in the process or activity. This variation may have been noted during the assessment fieldwork or later when evaluating the installed improvement. Variation is an important concept in statistics. Everyone is not the same height or weight. Highly trained personnel, using extremely prescriptive procedures, do not perform the same task exactly the same way every time. It is tempting to suggest that variation be minimized and reduced to zero if possible. This would be consistent with manufacturing (assembly line) concepts. However, this goal would not apply as well to surgery or claims adjustment. Accept that variation exists. The trick will be to ensure it is consistent with desired or acceptable limits.

Variation exists around some point or value, called the *norm* or *expected value*. Current thinking emphasizes considering variation first, then adjusting the norm once an acceptable value is reached. During the assessment and later on when evaluating installed improvements, this natural variation must be taken into account.

Varation is shown in Figure 9.1. Once performance moves into the natural variation band around the normal or prescribed level, point-to-point differences lose meaning.

Within the band, these differences occur strictly because of expected variation. There is no value in assigning any significance to their difference. (Pay no attention to the man behind the curtain.) Occurrences outside the band are usually either random in nature or due to assignable causes. They are usually easy to identify. What is important is determining the amount of natural variation that is acceptable. If the actual variation exceeds this amount, it is usually the system itself that must be changed.

This bends back on the original concept of valid rules and the degree of prescription appropriate to a given task or activity. It also affects what is being looked at. If the focus is on performance or effectiveness, what criteria are applied? How is variation defined and measured? The results are what is important; the technique less so. Only when the technique influences the outcome should it be considered. It does not matter what Albert Einstein was wearing or whether or not he was at the office when he came up with his theories. This is a big problem with many of the current performance indicators. They do not measure performance at all.

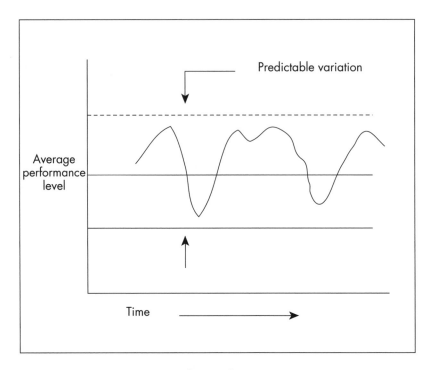

Figure 9.1
Random or non-assignable performance levels.

The remedy: When you look at variation, look at it in terms of performance or effectiveness. Factor in the specific situation and its importance. Examine it globally, not neighborhood by neighborhood. How different is it from the desired outcome?

10

Summary

No themes are so human as those that reflect for us, out of the confusion of life, the close connection of bliss and bale, of the things that help with the things that hurt, so dangling before us forever that bright hard metal, of so strange an alloy, one face of which is somebody's right and ease and the other somebody's pain and wrong.
—Henry James, *What Maisie Knew*

The following truisms are lifted from previous chapters. They are provided in summary fashion to reemphasize some of the advice and principles we believe are hard bright metal.

Some General Thoughts

To achieve world-class status, being good enough simply isn't. Companies that are running in place will almost surely lose direction and fail. Excellence is a moving target because customer expectations tend to increase. Effective competition will demand performance levels at new plateaus. To reach this new plateau, organizations will need to recognize and eventually adopt new management paradigms based on effective, collaborative efforts.

Issuing policy statements, devising slogans, putting up posters, writing commitment messages, or conducting rallies and meetings will not (by themselves) make these programs work. Several tools are needed to construct an effective TQM or continuous improvement program. They are different from the traditional tools of quality control (control charts, Pareto diagrams, flowcharting, and so on). The existing tools are not equal to the larger, more complex issues involved in the development and implementation of a TQM program. The newer elements to carry out an effective TQM program include

- Developing a means of defining customer expectations and translating these into realistic goals and objectives
- Using, developing, and empowering employees; treating these resources as capital
- Planning and espousing continuous improvement
- Developing and carrying out effective project and process management
- Using appropriate quantitative measurement techniques for status reporting and analysis of both positive and negative trends
- Developing an effective root cause analysis system to identify the real causes for organizational problems and identify the most obvious candidates for improvement
- Using positive fault correction; practical corrective, adaptive, and preventive actions

These basic systems need to be in place to make the program work. Without them, we have been sold a car without an engine; tasked to build an elaborate structure without materials, tools, or blueprints.

One of the realities of TQM or any improvement program is that personnel skills will require sharpening. Personnel will need to understand and be able to use a wider variety of analytical tools. Training should be viewed as an investment, not an expense. The real expense is less-than-optimal performance.

Delaying effectiveness or performance assessments, improved problem reporting systems, root cause analyses, and other similar systems makes no sense at all. In doing so, the organization is playing blindman's bluff. Even solid objects can disappear in the dark. If the organizational climate does not support or encourage improvement, the effort is wasted. Tacit approval is not sufficient endorsement. Until negative corporate inertia is overcome, little progress will be made. The easiest problem to solve is the one that does not occur. Anticipating and thereby avoiding problems is a higher level skill than solving them.

Organizations that have achieved some success cannot simply rest on their laurels. Disaster can be waiting around the next corner. It seems paradoxical that more effort will be required to solve problems, particularly when keeping up with them is difficult. However, it is the longer term perspective that is crucial.

Whether for reasons of competitiveness or to reduce potential liabilities, improved performance becomes an imperative. While defect-free performance is theoretically possible, it is accomplished only with constant diligence. If absolute perfection is difficult to achieve, much less maintain, then continuous improvement becomes the logical alternative. Improvement should not involve the questions why, what, or where. The only concerns should be how and when.

The Roles
All of us are both customers and suppliers. Our customers may be external or internal. The distinction between customer wants and needs must be made. All appropriate customer needs should be met or exceeded. Appropriate refers to discriminating these needs by importance and the particular situation. When you finally ask the right questions, listen carefully to the answers. Pay attention to the customer. Face the facts even if you don't like or agree with them.

Assessments in Particular
All important activities need to be planned, carried out, continuously assessed, and corrected as necessary to ensure continuous improvement. When the purpose of the assessment is important enough, there is no practical reason not to have accurate results. Assessment results that are dated, imprecise, ambiguous, or not reliable indicators of performance are of little or no value.

The assessed individual, group, or organization is the ultimate beneficiary of the assessment effort. They are the customer. Those who believe that the old way of conducting audits will suffice suffer the prospect of a rude awakening in a brave, new world.

Compliance-based assessments typically result in a listing of those items or areas observed which do not meet these predetermined requirements. The embedded assumption is that meeting these requirements is, of and by itself, sufficient and adequate. This may not be true.

Effectiveness or performance-based overview activities, properly conducted, require technical/program specialists or SMEs.

Corporate Culture

Corporate culture is broadly described as the organization's collective skills, shared values, and beliefs. It is evidenced by organizational policies, performance, established norms, and limits of behavior. Corporate culture often appears static, since it sometimes changes slowly. This phenomenon is referred to as *corporate inertia*. Corporate inertia can be a plus, once underway.

Corporate culture must first recognize the need for and then encourage continuous improvement. Performance assessments are necessary to measure and evaluate progress toward goals and objectives. A corporate culture that emphasizes conformity, hinders innovation, discourages bad news, or fails to recognize problems is a poor medium for the growth of an effective quality and productivity improvement program. The emphasis must be on the development and cultivation of a proactive, customer-oriented teamwork environment. Most companies find it worthwhile to examine their culture before launching any improvement program.

Organizations are comprised of interrelated groups and functions. Personnel act individually, as members of the group, and as components within the organization. Improvement starts with the individual. Through collective individual efforts, the team or group improves and, subsequently, so does the organization. While improvement must have top-level support, it occurs from the bottom up. This is the place to start.

Effective organization or team management results in strong performance and a shared vision of goals and objectives. There may be a need to flex current organizational constraints to allow for individual and group growth. When looking at rules, pay particular attention to their relationship to performance. Install and follow rules only when absolutely necessary. Limit the number and complexity of rules. Substitute goals and objectives for rules.

Team Play

All organizational activities should recognize the importance of team play. Like a winning rowing team, all members of the organization must be pulling in unison and steer a steady, true course to the finish line. You can look back to see how steady the effort has been. It also helps to look around to see how the other teams are doing. But most importantly, look ahead toward the finish line.

When the focus and emphasis is on performance and continuous improvement, individuals within the corporate culture respond positively. They quickly discover that reliance on others is needed to reach goals. Collaborations will naturally establish themselves. A sense of team play will spontaneously emerge.

Each member of the team must measure and rate his or her own performance in relation to not only his or her own, but the group's goals and objectives. This revised concept suggests that efforts be directed toward helping others succeed. Those less inclined toward altruism should realize that when the team (organization) wins, they do too.

Situational conditions play a more important role when performance is less strictly prescribed. Minimally acceptable performance standards must be set. While many companies contend that they already have these, most fall short of the mark. Achieving these standards is the responsibility of the entire organization, from the top executives to individual contributors. Definition and consistent interpretation of performance expectations are crucial.

Improvement involves learning. The organization needs to foster a no-fault attitude toward this learning process. Personnel should freely identify needed improvements.

Performance improvement proceeds bottom up. Once started, it flows to the group and organization. If this flow is diverted or stopped altogether, the progression will obviously not occur. Until the corporate culture is opportune, improvement efforts will be wasted. Only when the organizational climate is favorable will meaningful performance improvement occur.

The Setting

Performance that meets or exceeds customer expectations is good business sense. When sufficient attention is given to the customer, benefits will accrue to the company. Optimal performance is doing exactly what is needed, depending on the situation and its importance.

Undue emphasis is often placed on conformance to established norms. Norm-based, rather than criteria-referenced or performance-based strategies are probably the most insidious concept ever fostered. Acceptance of the previous norm has several basic embedded flaws which include that it is static, that it will always be satisfactory, and that there will always be sufficient time and allowances made for any corrections if they become necessary.

Realistic improvement plans must continuously factor in the understood limitations of the current process. It is unrealistic to set improvement targets that cannot be obtained. As these improvements or changes are introduced, appropriate quantitative and/or qualitative feedback measures must also be installed to measure progress and ensure that the goals are first met and then maintained. Accept that variation exists. The trick will be to ensure it is consistent with desired or acceptable limits. If actual variation exceeds these limits, it is usually the system itself that must be changed.

Failure to act on needed improvements is worse than not recognizing the need for them in the first place because considerable effort and time will have been expended for no worthwhile purpose.

Strategy

Performance-based assessments are unnecessary for relatively straightforward activities with minimum operational impact. Use them for that class of issues called showstoppers. Adoption of a graded approach will influence selecting the assessment type. The assessment effort should fit the situation and its importance. Find out about and fix the things that are really wrong first; return to those of lesser importance later.

Effectiveness and performance assessments aim for improvement. The tone should be prospective, not protagonistic. If problems or unwanted conditions are found, treat them objectively. Problems are everyone's responsibility, even if they appear to surface in one area. Even apparently trivial problems can affect the overall operation and result in inefficiencies and customer dissatisfaction. Trivial problems often combine or grow to become major problems. Effective problem solving ensures that issues are correctly tagged.

Overall organizational improvement is sometimes best accomplished by a series of smaller wins rather than hoping for one large victory. Use evolution rather than revolution. Success breeds success. Find those areas that everybody thinks need fixing. First, you have built-in support. You also have a predisposition to change. Start with a group anxious to improve. A willing partner is important. Use the results as a demonstration to others. Let the successful group members be your salespeople. Find target-rich environments for assessments.

Customers should participate in the assessment efforts. It is their particular activities that will be improved. They are motivated. Their input to the analysis virtually guarantees their acceptance and carrying out of the results. Teamwork and collaboration are effective means to ensure a successful outcome. Performance can be individual or collective, but it always is played against some background.

Find the pulse points, those particular places where operation of the system is most easily measured. To get to the real issues, we must go further than identifying symptoms. Remember that in most of the cases (80 percent or better) of less-than-adequate performance or failure to improve, the system is at fault.

The only rational basis for an assisted self-assessment is training, that is, helping others to succeed. The three types of assessments are largely a matter of perspective. Objectivity and independence of view are characteristics which may be evidenced in any type of assessment. Given the variety of types and assessment approaches available, it is important to achieve the right mix. The mix of external, internal, and self-assessments and the types will vary depending on the situation.

Performance-Based Assessments—Planning

Performance-based assessments should not be conducted unless at least one hoped-for positive outcome is identified. Ensure that the assessed organization clearly understands this purpose, scope, and intent. Encourage everyone's full participation. When benefits are listed, they should accrue to the customer. The ultimate success of the effort is judged by a simple criteria: Did we find some way to do things better?

Effective planning is the key to eventual success. Any productivity or quality improvement program requires long-term organizational commitment. Experience suggests that less-than-adequate planning is the prime cause of most organizational problems.

Many activities or processes are unnecessarily (and expensively) constrained by full compliance to broad standards. When the assessment is based on effectiveness or performance, comments regarding the validity of any and all requirements are allowed, even encouraged.

Planning for effectiveness and performance-based assessments is quite different from the detailed checklisting effort associated with compliance overviews. It is more accurately a listing of potential areas of interest (which may be revised or expanded upon) during the actual fieldwork. The assessment plan can be changed. Results are more important than how well the plan was followed.

Measuring performance characteristics is difficult unless quantifiable criteria have been established during the planning stage. It is particularly hard to do when people or values are involved.

The choice of the team leader is by far the most crucial ingredient for success in a performance-based assessment. Success is directly related to the process familiarity and experience of the team members. All team members should have the ability to see the forest instead of the trees. They need to be able to see what is really happening. Team selection is based on the type of assessment, activity or process, and the scope. Members of the team should be selected primarily on their expertise.

The assessment team must establish clear intent, define the scope along activity lines, ensure technical competence, foster a team approach, emphasize improvement, and be professional and objective. Administrative and scheduling considerations should encourage participation in the assessment efforts by the organization, group, or individual being evaluated.

Performance objectives, where they exist, can be used to directly plan assessments. If performance objectives are not stated, the team must devise them. Both stretch and expected improvement goals should be identified.

Performance-Based Assessments—Conduct

The team leader's role is more a referee, catalyst, and trainer than anything else. Effectiveness and performance-based assessments require a more disciplined, technically competent approach. Fieldwork for an effectiveness or performance-based assessment takes more time and work.

When a serious issue surfaces, available time and resources should be spent determining the real cause rather than searching for additional examples of the same problem. The fieldwork should gather sufficient information to allow an effective root cause analysis to be performed later on any surfaced problems or unwanted conditions. Some expertise must be team-resident or otherwise available during the planning and fieldwork to guide this effort.

Performance-based assessments require direct observation and evaluation of the process or activity. In a performance-based assessment, the team must look beyond compliance issues and evaluate both operational effectiveness and performance.

The primary focus should be on characteristics important in the particular situation. Forget lesser issues. Concentrate on the significant ones that have been identified. The actual fieldwork is as important as the planning. Assessors must carefully observe all that is going on. Look for patterns or groups, rather than specific instances. Identify all undocumented activities and self-correcting mechanisms. Good fieldwork makes the later analysis and framing of results easy. However, it is difficult to predict accurately how long the fieldwork will take.

Performance-Based Assessments—Results

Auditors can make recommendations. Sound conclusions resulting from the assessment are the crown jewels of the effort. They should flow logically from the planned goals and later fieldwork. Compliance, effectiveness, and performance issues should be separated during the analysis and in the final report.

The findings and results need to be prioritized, primarily by significance. Sideways looks are needed to frame most performance issues. The extent of needed or possible improvement must be realistically bounded. Every issue or improvement opportunity identified must be sufficiently developed to be able to identify its true nature and extent.

In devising potential solutions, cover the entire range from the most obvious to the most creative. Collective thinking (groupthink in 1960s terms) will result in a predictably better outcome. Don't limit individual contribution. Encourage all input. Use benchmarking to find out what others have done in similar situations. Borrow or stretch ideas. Elegant solutions sometimes come from areas or disciplines outside our immediate area of expertise. Develop a wider view. Avoid unnecessary restrictions.

Evaluate solutions in terms of whether they are long- versus short-term and targeted versus generic. Are they targeted to the specific issue or represent a broader, more generic solution? Look at any proposed solution in terms of the importance of the issue and the particular situation. Recognize that what works well in one situation may be entirely inadequate in another. Make sure all proposed improvements have a clear statement with the essential features identified, well-defined attributes and characteristics, and qualitative or quantitative measures for evaluation.

Frame every issue by its effect on operation or performance. Capture the essence of the proposed solution. Solutions should relate directly to planned goals. Review each potential solution with the affected organization. Alternative approaches should have only one ultimate decision criterion: Will it produce the desired result?

All plans should contain evaluation criteria. These are vital to providing a measure of progress or accomplishment. If the improvement plan has none, add them. The improvement plan should include a reasonably accurate inventory of the resources needed to carry it out. The resource loading should identify person-hours, budget, training requirements, situational factors, and so on.

Make sure the improvement is fully developed. Do your homework first. Use a systems approach to improvement. Create a vision of the planned improvement in place. Describe the improvement in positive terms. Involve affected individuals. Develop incentives. Provide training.

Change and its effects must be factored into the development and presentation of the improvement plan. While the proposed change can be evaluated solely on its inherent merit, the planning and implementation effort also needs to be measured and judged in terms of its adequacy. Recognize that problems can arise during the implementation phase. Many will be no one in particular's fault. The idea just needs further refinement. Follow-through is a nurturing process, one of ensuring that the improvement is moving forward as planned. If difficulties are encountered, these obstacles must be removed.

Use criteria that are based more on results than the mechanics of the system. Judge the actual improvement based on achievement. Look at substance, rather than form. Focus on the results. Have we increased client satisfaction? Are we doing better? Are we recognizing and solving problems in a timely and effective manner? Are we preventing their recurrence?

Any improvement, when first installed, is likely to contain some embedded flaws. Do not allow this to be the reason for delay. When unexpected flaws emerge, do not disregard them. Use them to fine-tune the system. Recognize that effective systems evolve and were not created that way.

The Need for Continuous Improvement

In writing this book, our intention was to present an overview of continuous improvement concepts and some of the techniques that can be used to provide accurate measurement and assessment. We started by defining performance. This included meeting or exceeding customers' expectations in relation to their importance in the particular situation.

We have presented a number of ideas and suggestions. Our intention in doing so was, of course, to demonstrate the variety of assessment types and strategies that are available, rather than endorse one method over the other. Throughout the book, we have emphasized the graded approach. Choose the method and type assessment which fits the importance or, alternately, the consequences of ineffectiveness, less-than-adequate performance or misperformance.

Throughout the chapters, we have stressed the positive, prospective use of assessments. We believe this to be the surest road to individual, group, and organizational improvement.

The Malcolm Baldrige National Quality Award

The Malcolm Baldrige National Quality Award, named for the late U.S. Secretary of Commerce, was established by act of Congress in 1987. The goals of this award are to promote quality awareness, recognize quality leadership and achievement, and publicize successful quality strategies. Organizations are graded on

- Leadership in creating and maintaining a quality culture
- The effectiveness of information and analysis in planning quality
- Strategic quality planning
- Effective human resource utilization
- Quality assurance activities
- Quality achievement and improvement
- Customer satisfaction

Readers will no doubt note the similarity of these items with concepts discussed previously in this book as well as the basic premise of an effective TQM program.

Process and Activity Improvement

Throughout the book, we have pointed out the need for continuous process or activity improvement. We have also stressed that it is difficult to improve a process or activity if you do not understand how it operates. You cannot hope to reduce inconsistencies if you have no idea of the inherent variation of the process. Assessments must be linked to the other needed elements of TQM, such as effective process project/process management (which include process capability studies, analysis and reduction of variance, and so on), fault correction, root cause analyses, trend analysis, and so forth. Effective assessments are only one piece of the puzzle. While vital elements of any quality and productivity program, assessments are most effective when used in conjunction with the pieces of the puzzle that are also needed.

A Final Word

Readers who have followed the book thus far may be dismayed at the fact that, despite all that may have been done, more work still lies ahead. If organizations do not get started and keep going, they will be left behind. Questioning and constant change forms the basis for our culture. This heritage can be traced to the ancient Greeks. For us new or improved means better. No further explanation is required.

In like manner, we love change, at least in some things. Better also means different. We look forward to and expect change in many things. Who would buy the automobile billed as exactly like last year's model? Curiously, however, there is a comfort baseline of things we like to change only slowly or not at all. There are also things we like to see change, but don't. So we have a curious mix; a love-hate relationship.

There is inertia involved with change of any kind. Perhaps more so with a radical departure from the way things have been done before. There probably will be some discomfort, even some genuine pain. But on the other hand, there also exists some fertile ground in which to plant changed concepts

People are tired of the same old problems, of constantly trying to catch up, and are convinced there must be better ways of doing things. Many are receptive, at least at the gut level, to meaningful change. This happens a lot in politics.

Change has two aspects: the merit of the proposed change and the means of implementing these changes. Given that the change will result in some improvement, the means used to carry it out will be important. Quality circles were largely doomed to failure because organizations failed to listen to, consider, and implement the recommended actions. Similarly, root cause analyses are largely ineffective in organizations which do not accurately identify faults and problems, provide less-than-adequate analyses because of poor staffing or training, or fail to act on proposed solutions or translate the results into more palatable solutions, regardless of their merit. Effectiveness and performance-based assessments likewise will fall short of their promise if improvement is not really wanted. Perhaps, like the recovering alcoholic, these organizations must first declare openly that they have a problem.

The authors believe that all that has been included in these chapters is vitally important. This book could have been subtitled "Helping Others Succeed" since this is also true. We have stressed a positive tone for assessments with a view to improvement. Recognize that the desire for improvement must be internalized first. As the previous paragraph suggests, the main problem may be in convincing others that opportunities for improvement exist.

We have attempted to apply reasonable balance to this effort by suggesting a graded approach. Some problems are not worth fixing at all. For others, adaptive strategies may be appropriate: sort of like driving around the potholes. We have also cautioned that most opportunities for improvement are embedded in the processes and activities themselves. Only their modification will ultimately result in the desired outcome.

We have no doubt created some anxieties. One might be that we are not doing all we could reasonably do to improve our present operations. We have given you some tools and then told you that their use is up to you. We have attempted to show the importance of effectiveness and performance-based assessments as vital elements in any continuous improvement program, such as TQM. In addition to all this information and advice, we have to add the final, unequivocal argument in support of our thesis: We know effectiveness and performance-based assessments will work because we have seen them work. They can work for you as well.

Suggested Reading

Arter, Dennis R. *Quality Audits for Improved Performance*, 2d ed. Milwaukee, Wis.: ASQC Quality Press, 1994.

Barrow, James W. "Does Total Quality Management Equal Organizational Learning?" *Quality Progress* (July 1993): 39–43.

Corcoran, William R., James E. Gieger, Richard P. Heibel, John B. Cotton, and Andrew R. Sabol. "Nuclear Quality Assurance Operating Philosophy—A Quality-Oriented Approach." *Nuclear Plant Journal* (August 1992): 88–90.

Cottman, Ronald J. *A Guidebook to ISO 9000 and ANSI/ASQC Q90*. Milwaukee, Wis.: ASQC Quality Press, 1993.

Fenwick, Alan C. "Five Easy Lessons." *Quality Progress* (December 1991): 63–66.

GAO/NSIAD-91-190. "U.S. Companies Improve Performance Through Quality Efforts." Washington, D.C.: U.S. General Accounting Office, 1991.

Gaudard, Marie, Ronald Coates, and Liz Freeman. "Accelerating Improvement." *Quality Progress* (October 1991): 81–88.

Gore, Al. *From Red Tape to Results: Creating a Government That Works Better and Costs Less*. Report of the National Performance Review. Washington, D.C.: Government Printing Office, 1993.

Graber, Jim M., Roger E. Breisch, and Walter E. Breisch. "Performance Appraisals and Deming: A Misunderstanding?" *Quality Progress* (June 1992): 59–62.

Juran, J. M. "Strategies for World-Class Quality." *Quality Progress* (March 1991): 81–85.

———. "The Cost of Quality." *Newsweek* (September 7, 1992): 48–49.

Kinni, Theodore B. "Benchmarking: One Measurement in the Continuous Improvement Process." *Quality Digest* (November 1993): 24–29.

Morgan, Ronald B. and Jack E. Smith. "A New Era in Manufacturing and Service." *Quality Progress* (July 1993): 83–89.

Peters, Thomas and Robert Waterman, Jr. *In Search of Excellence: Lessons from America's Best-Run Companies.* New York: Harper & Row, 1982.

Russell, J. P. "Six-Point Quality Planning." *Quality Progress* (April 1991): 55–58.

Saraph, Jayant V. and Richard J. Sebastion. "Developing a Quality Culture." *Quality Progress* (September 1993): 73–78.

Scalpone, Russell W. "Assessing Quality Improvement." *Quality Digest* (November 1993): 50–55.

Schwartz, M. H. "A Question of Semantics." *Quality Progress* (November 1991): 59–63.

———. "What Do the Words 'Product' and 'Service' Really Mean for Management?" *Quality Progress* (June 1992): 35–39.

Shores, A. Richard. "Improving the Quality of Management Systems." *Quality Progress* (June 1992): 53–57.

Slater, Roger H. "Integrated Process Management: A Quality Model." *Quality Progress* (May 1991): 75–80.

Smith, A. Keith. "Total Quality Management in the Public Sector, Part 1." *Quality Progress* (June 1993): 45–48.

Spitzer, Richard D. "TQM: The Only Source of Sustainable Competitive Advantage." *Quality Progress* (June 1993): 59–64.

Stuelpnagel, Thomas R. "Integrated Product Management." *Quality Digest* (June 1993): 39–47.

Wilson, Paul F., Larry Dell, and Gaylord Anderson. *Root Cause Analysis: A Tool for Total Quality Management.* Milwaukee, Wis.: ASQC Quality Press, 1993.

Index